ORLANDO TRAVEL GUIDE 2024

Ultimate Guide to Walt Disney World & Universal Orlando Resort, LEGOLAND, etc. With Tips On Best Places to Visit, Travel Budget, Multichoiced Itineraries, Tips and Tricks.

Jette Florence &
Edited by: John J. Bartel

Disclaimer: The prices for activities and services written in this guide are approximate, in that the world economy changes at large and prices fluctuate. But they definitely give you an insight on how you would spend the course of your vacation in Orlando.

ORLANDO TRAVEL GUIDE 2024
(1st Edition)

TABLE OF CONTENTS

Chapter 1.. **8**

Hello And welcome To Orlando...................... **8**

   About This Guide Book............................... 8

   An Overview of Orlando............................. 9

Chapter 2.. **11**

Making Your Travel Plans......................... **11**

   When Should You Visit Orlando?.............. 11

   Climate and Weather................................ 11

   Peak Travel Seasons................................ 13

   Essential Travel Requirements................. 15

   Currency and Money Matters................... 17

   Itinerary Planning.................................. 21

Chapter 3.. **29**

Exploring the Neighborhoods of Orlando....... **29**

   Downtown Orlando.................................. 29

   I-Drive (International Drive)..................... 32

   The ICON Park....................................... 33

   I-Drive shopping.................................... 35

Chapter 4.. **38**

Major Theme Parks and Attractions.............. **38**

Walt Disney World Resort........................ **39**

   The Magic Kingdom................................ 39

   Epcot World of Discovery......................... 41

   Hollywood Studios at Disney.................... 43

   Disney's Animal Kingdom........................ 44

   Disney Springs...................................... 46

Universal Orlando Resort........................ **47**

   The Universal Studios Florida.................. 47

   Attractions And Thrill Rides.................... 49

SeaWorld Orlando................................... **51**

SeaWorld Theme Park..51

Discovery Cove... 53

Aquatica Theme Park.. 54

LEGOLAND Florida Resort............................. 56

LEGOLAND Theme Park.. 56

LEGOLAND Water Park.. 58

Kennedy Space Center Visitor Complex........... 60

Rocket Garden..60

Space Shuttle Atlantis.. 60

Shuttle Launch Experience......................................61

Astronaut Encounter.. 61

The IMAX Theater.. 61

Rocket Launch Viewing...62

Space Center Bus Tour..62

Educational Opportunities.......................................62

Practical Information.. 63

Dining and Souvenirs...64

I-Drive ICONic Attractions............................65

Madame Tussauds Orlando..................................... 65

The Wheel at ICON Park...66

Ripley's Believe It or Not!.......................................67

Kissimmee And Beyond.................................. 68

Kissimmee's Historic District.................................. 68

Gatorland...69

Wildlife and Nature Preserves................................. 70

Chapter 5..72

Outdoor Adventures.....................................72

Central Florida Parks... 72

Wekiwa Springs State Park..................................... 72

Blue Spring State Park..75

The Manatee Sanctuary...76

Ocala National Forest...78

Airboat Tours In The Everglades..............................81
Hot Air Ballooning..83
Kayaking and Canoeing Expeditions.......................84
Golfin' Orlando...86
Segway Tours And Biking Trails..............................89

Chapter 6.. **92**

Arts And Culture... **92**
Orlando Museum of Art (OMA)...............................92
Dr. Phillips Center For Performing Arts.................95
Charles Hosmer Morse Museum of American Art..98
Harry P. Leu Gardens... 101
Mennello Museum of American Art...................... 104
Shakespeare Theater.. 107

Chapter 7.. **112**

Dining and Culinary Delights........................ **112**
The Culinary Scene in Orlando..............................112
International Cuisines..112
Local Favorites.. 114
Food Trucks and Street Eats..................................116
Fine Dining and Upscale Restaurants................... 117
Vegetarian and Vegan Options.............................. 119
Craft Beer and Breweries....................................... 120
Wineries and Distilleries.. 122

Chapter 8..**125**

Nightlife And Entertainment......................... **125**
Nightlife in Downtown Orlando.............................125
The International Drive Entertainment.................127
Themed Dinner Shows.. 128
Live Music Venues... 129
Comedy Clubs.. 130
Nightclubs and Bars... 132
Family-Friendly Evening Activities........................134

Chapter 9..**136**
Shopping And Getting Around......................**136**
    Shoppin' Orlando................................136
    Shopping Districts.................................. 136
    Souvenirs And Gifts................................139
    Getting Around Orlando...................... 140
    Transportation Alternatives...................140
    Public Transportation............................142
    Cycling and walking..............................143
    Tourist Safety Recommendations.......... 143

Chapter 10..**146**
Practical Informations..................................**146**
    Emergency Contacts...............................146
    Orlando Health......................................146
    Visitor Information Centers...................149

Appendices...**151**
    Sample Itineraries................................151
    (3 Days) Family Adventure...................... 151
    (2 Days) Getaway for Thrill-Seekers...... 154
    Theme Park Ticket Informations........... 155
    Festivals and Annual Events.................. 159

Chapter 1

Hello And welcome To Orlando

Welcome to the enchanted city of Orlando, Florida, where fantasies come true and enjoyment has no bounds. Dubbed "The Theme Park Capital of the World," Orlando is an enthralling destination recognized for its world-class attractions, entertainment, magnificent beauty and lively culture.

Orlando serves as the true stimulant for kids fantasy, and there's no better way to make colorful memories with your kids than at these magical and out of earth color land!

About This Guide Book

This guide will take you on a tour into the heart of Orlando, while offering you vital insights, recommendations, and tips to make your vacation absolutely memorable, because you deserve it! Together, we will look at everything Orlando has to offer, from its major theme parks to its hidden jewels, food, family-friendly alternatives, retail areas, thrilling activities and much more.

This guide is designed to be your ultimate essential companion whether you are a first-time tourist or have been to Orlando before.

We have compiled a variety of information to assist you in properly planning your vacation, making the most of your time, and ensuring that your Orlando experience is nothing short of wonderful.

In this guide is a compilation of information variety to assist you in properly planning your vacation, making the most of your time, and ensuring that your Orlando experience is nothing short of wonderful.

An Overview of Orlando

Orlando is located in central Florida, making it conveniently accessible from major cities throughout the United States! It has an area of around 294 square miles (762 square kilometers) and is recognized for having lush landscapes and numerous lakes, which contribute to its natural beauty.

Orlando has a subtropical climate with hot, humid summers and mild winters. In that note when planning your trip, it is critical to keep the weather in mind and also allow the weather to influence your activities and clothing Choices for an overall enjoyable stay. Temperatures in the winter range from 70°F (21°C) to 92°F (33°C) in the summer.

Orlando has a population of around 290,000 people. However, due to the influx of tourists, especially during peak holiday seasons, this figure can greatly fluctuate.

Language: ***English*** is the most often spoken language in Orlando, although due to the city's diverse population, you may hear other languages, including ***Spanish*** and ***Portuguese***.

Currency

The United States *Dollar (USD)* is the currency that's in use in Orlando. Credit and debit cards are frequently accepted, however carry extra cash with you for little transactions and situations where cards may not be accepted.

Time Zone

Orlando is in the Eastern Time Zone (ET), which is UTC-5 during Standard Time and UTC-4 during Daylight Saving Time (observed from the second Sunday in March to the first Sunday in November).

Getting Around: Rental cars, taxis, rideshare services like Uber and Lyft, public buses, and even a commuter train system called SunRail are available in Orlando. We will go over transportation in greater detail later in this guide book.

Chapter 2

Making Your Travel Plans

When Should You Visit Orlando?

The time you choose to visit Orlando might have a major impact on your whole vacation experience. Orlando, Florida, is a popular tourist destination all year, but recognizing the seasons and their implications will help you make the most of your visit.

This chapter will go through the numerous considerations and options to consider while arranging a trip to the Sunshine State.

Climate and Weather

Orlando has a subtropical climate, with hot and humid summers, mild winters, and moderate rainfall throughout the year. Understanding Orlando' weather patterns might assist you in packing wisely and planning your activities.

Summer months (June to August)

Summers in Orlando are notorious for their high temperatures and humidity. Average highs of up to 90° Fahrenheit (32-37°C) are possible.

In Orlando thunderstorms are common in the afternoon, so be prepared for unexpected rain showers.

During this season, popular activities include visiting water parks such as Walt Disney World's Typhoon Lagoon and Blizzard Beach and Hotel costs in the mid-range range between $150 and $300 per night.

Autumn (September-November)

The weather in Orlando begins to cool down in the fall, with average temperatures ranging from the mid-70s to the low 80s Fahrenheit (24-29°C).

Crowds are often thinner, making popular attractions easier to appreciate. During this season, Halloween-themed events at numerous theme parks are a highlight.

Hotel costs in the mid-range range between $100 to $250 per night.

From December until February

Orlando's winters are mild and pleasant, with temperatures averaging in the 60s and 70s Fahrenheit (15-24° Celsius).

This is a popular season for theme park holiday parties, such as Mickey's Very Merry Christmas Party at Disney World. The lower crowds in comparison to the summer months make it an appealing time to visit.

Hotel costs in the mid-range range between $100 to $300 per night.

From March until May

Spring in Orlando is distinguished by mild temperatures and low humidity, making it an ideal season to visit the city.

At Disney World, the Epcot International Flower & Garden Festival is a notable springtime event. Spring break might be crowded, so prepare appropriately.

Hotel costs in the mid-range range from $150 to $350 per night.

Peak Travel Seasons

Understanding Orlando's high tourist seasons is critical for controlling crowds and expenses during your visit. While Orlando welcomes visitors all year, some times of the year see a substantial influx of tourists, this includes:

Summer Vacation (June to August)

Schools are out, and families are flocking to Orlando, resulting in overcrowding and increased wait times at amusement parks. During this season, lodging prices tend to be on the higher side.

Thanksgiving, Christmas, and New Year (Festival Seasons Of The Year)

The holiday events in Orlando are well-known, but they also bring enormous crowds. Make eating and event bookings well in advance during these hours. During the holiday season, hotel prices may rise.

Spring Break (March-April)

College students and families on vacation flock to Orlando, increasing demand for lodging.

Popular destinations can get packed, so plan your vacation cautiously around these busy times.

Festivals and Special Events (Varies)

Throughout the year, Orlando holds a variety of events, such as the Epcot Food & Wine Festival.
These events may result in increased hotel prices and foot traffic.

It is important that when arranging your trip to Orlando, you keep the weather, climate, and peak tourist seasons in mind to ensure a more enjoyable and cost-effective visit. You may choose the optimal time for your Orlando journey based on your tastes, whichever festivities you want to attend and as well as tolerance for crowds.

Essential Travel Requirements

Entry and Visa Requirements

Before starting on an international trip, it is critical to grasp your destination's visa and admission procedures. These criteria might differ greatly from one country to the next, so it is critical to do your homework ahead of time. Consider the following crucial points:

Visa Categories

Tourist Visa: Most visitors choose a tourist visa, which allows them to visit a nation for a set period of time, often ranging from a few weeks to several months. (This is the most recommended for your trip to Orlando).

Business Visa: If you intend to conduct business, attend conferences, or work briefly in a foreign country, you may require a business visa.

Student Visa: A student visa is required if you are traveling overseas for educational purposes, such as attending a university or language school.

Transit visas are required if you have a layover in a country and need to leave the airport for any reason.

Entry Requirements

Entry requirements may include the following:

Validity of Passport: Make sure your passport is valid for at least six months beyond your scheduled departure date.

Visa Application: Learn about the visa application procedure for your destination, which may include filling out forms, submitting supporting documentation, and paying fees.

Visa Processing Time: Plan ahead of time because visa processing times might vary greatly. Some visas are processed in a matter of days, while others may take several weeks.

Visa fees can range from as little as $20 for some countries to more than $200 for others, so endeavor to check out the fee from your current destination or country appropriately.

Visa Exemption

Some nations have agreements that allow tourists to enter for a certain time without a visa. As an example:

Schengen Area: The Schengen Area is a group of European countries that allows people to roam freely between member countries with a single visa.

Visa Waiver Program (VWP): The United States allows people of specified nations to enter the country without a visa for tourism or commercial purposes.

For the most up-to-date visa requirements, always consult the official government website of your destination (in this case Orlando) or the nearest embassy or consulate.

Currency and Money Matters

Understanding the currency and managing your cash while traveling are critical for a successful vacation. Consider the following crucial points:

Money Exchange Rates: Monitor exchange rates and select a favorable moment to swap your money. Exchange rates might change on a daily basis.

Exchange Options: Foreign currency can be exchanged in banks, currency exchange agencies, or even ATMs. To locate the best deal, compare rates and fees.

Payment Methods

Currency Prepaid Cards: Consider purchasing a **prepaid currency card** that enables you to load different currencies into a single card. This can save you money on currency exchange expenses.

Credit and Debit Cards: Inform your bank of your travel plans in order to avoid problems with your credit or debit cards while overseas. Keep an eye out for overseas transaction costs.

Cash vs. Card Emergency Money: Always keep some cash in the local currency on hand for emergencies, especially for locations where card acceptance might be limited.

Card Security: Keep your cards and PINs safe. To prevent digital theft, use RFID-blocking wallets.

Travel Budgeting: Ensure to make a travel budget for your trip, including daily spending for meals, transportation, and activities. This will allow you to better manage your funds.

Accommodation Options

Choosing the proper lodging is an important component of your journey planning. Your options for accommodation in Orlando ranges from low-cost hostels to opulent resorts. Take a look at them as follows:

Luxury Stays

Luxury hotels provide first-rate amenities such as spa treatments, excellent cuisine, and concierge services. Prices each night might range from $200 to $1,000 or more.

Mid-Range Hotels: Mid-range hotels are comfortable and well-equipped, and normally cost between $80 and $200 per night.
Budget Hotels: Low-cost hotels ranging from $30 to $80 a night.

Additional Accommodations

Hostels: Hostels are ideal for budget tourists, they provide both dormitory-style and private rooms if you want. Prices vary, but can range from $10 to $50 each night.

Vacation Rentals: Platforms such as Airbnb offer a diverse selection of rental alternatives, ranging from apartments to houses. Prices vary according to location and amenities.

Camping: If you enjoy being outside, camping can be a cost-effective option. The cost of a campsite varies greatly plan according to your budget.

Booking Sites

Compare current costs, read reviews, and book your hotel in advance using booking sites such as Booking.com, Expedia, or TripAdvisor.
It is best to book ahead of time, especially during peak travel seasons.

Packing Suggestions

Packing efficiently can make your trip more comfortable and stress-free. Here's how to pack efficiently:

Checklisting for Packing

Make a list of everything: Make a packing list to ensure you do not forget anything important, such as clothing, toiletries, and travel documents.

Luggage

Choosing the Best Bag: Choose luggage that is appropriate for your travel style, whether it be a backpack, suitcase, or duffel bag.

Pro Tip;

Pack Light!: To avoid unnecessary baggage costs and to make traveling easier, pack only what you need.

On Clothing...

Versatile Clothing: Bring clothing that can be mixed and matched to produce a variety of outfits that Carter for the warm and humid weather in Orlando.

Make Considerations for the Weather: Check the weather forecast before you leave for Orlando and pack accordingly.

Travel Equipments

Travel Adapters: Bring the appropriate power adapters for the US region with you to charge your electronics.

There are two associated plug types for the United States: A and B. The plug type A has two flat parallel pins, while the plug type B has two flat parallel pins and a grounding pin. The United States uses a 120V supply voltage and a 60Hz frequency.

Even though there are now compact adapters with multiple different outlets, it is advisable to come the generally used type in the region for easier access to electricity.

Travel-Sized Toiletries: To reduce room and comply with flight requirements, use travel-sized toiletries.

Travel Locks: Use TSA-approved locks to secure your luggage.

With these travel necessities in mind, you will be well-prepared for your trip, ensuring a smooth and enjoyable voyage. Remember that careful planning and research can considerably improve your vacation experience.

Itinerary Planning

When planning a vacation to Orlando, one of Florida's most popular tourist attractions, it is critical to plan ahead of time to make the most of your time there. Orlando has a wide choice of experiences to suit a variety of interests and inclinations.

In this section, we will look at different itinerary possibilities for families with children, couples looking for a romantic break, theme park fans, outdoor adventurers, culture aficionados, foodies, and those eager to experience the city's dynamic nightlife.

Family-Friendly Orlando

Orlando is well-known for its family-friendly attractions, making it an ideal getaway for families. Here are some must-see destinations and activities for families:

- *Walt Disney wonderland Resort*: No trip to Orlando is complete without a visit to Disney's enchanted wonderland. Magic Kingdom, Epcot, Disney's Hollywood Studios, and Disney's Animal Kingdom are the four primary theme parks. A single-day ticket costs roughly $109 per person.

- *Universal Orlando Resort*: Immerse yourself in Harry Potter's wizarding world at

Universal's Islands of Adventure and Universal Studios Florida. A two-park, one-day ticket costs around $170 per person.

- *LEGOLAND Florida Resort*: Ideal for younger children who enjoy LEGO, LEGOLAND Florida Resort features rides, shows, and a water park. A single-day pass starts at $74.99 per person.

- *Kennedy Space Center Visitor Complex*: A fun and instructive event for the entire family. Tickets cost between $47 to $57 per person.

Couples Getaway

Consider the following activities and locations for a romantic getaway in Orlando:

- *Hot Air Balloon Ride*: For a genuinely romantic experience, soar above the lovely surroundings of Central Florida. Prices vary, but typically begins at $175 per person.

- *Luxury Resorts*: Stay at an upscale resort in Orlando, such as the Waldorf Astoria or Four Seasons. Prices start at $300 per night and rise from there.

- *Fine Dining*: Treat your significant other to a romantic dinner at a high-end restaurant such as Victoria & Albert's, where tasting menus start at roughly $185 per person.

- *Scenic Boat trip*: A scenic boat trip, which normally costs around $14 per person, allows you to explore the natural beauty of Orlando's lakes and canals.

- *Dr. Phillips Center for the Performing Arts*: Take in a Broadway performance or a concert as a group. The cost of tickets varies based on the event.

Theme Park Enthusiast

Orlando is a great destination for theme park enthusiasts, with multiple world-class parks to explore. Here are some tips and cheat codes for an optimal Theme Park experience:

- *Multi-Day Park Hopper Tickets*: For the most flexibility, choose multi-day park hopper tickets, which allow you to visit various parks in a single day. Prices vary depending on the number of days and parks you want to visit.

- *FastPasses*: Consider purchasing FastPasses to avoid long lineups and maximize your time. Depending on the park and activities, prices range from $15 to $199 per person.

- *VIP Tours*: For an enhanced experience, certain parks provide VIP tours. For example, the VIP Experience at Universal Orlando starts at around $189 per person.

- *Tips on Special Events*: Keep an eye out for special events that may incur additional fees, such as Halloween Horror Nights at Universal or Epcot's Food and Wine Festival ect.

Outdoor Adventure

These natural surroundings of Orlando offer numerous options for outdoor enthusiasts:

- *Kayaking*: For a peaceful paddle on one of Orlando's many lakes, rent kayaks for roughly $15 per hour.

- *Biking*: Rent a bike for $10 to $20 per hour and explore the West Orange Trail or other attractive biking paths in the vicinity.

- *Ziplining*: Enjoy the excitement of ziplining at Gatorland's Screamin' Gator Zip Line, which starts at around $70 per person.

- *Eco Tours*: Take an eco-tour to learn about Florida's unique fauna and ecosystems. Prices vary depending on the tour operator and the length of the trip.

- *Gatorland*: Get up close and personal with alligators and other creatures at this attraction. Adult tickets are roughly $29.99 while children's tickets are around $19.99.

Arts and Culture

Orlando has a variety of museums and cultural activities for individuals interested in the arts and culture, these includes:

- *Orlando Museum of Art*: Admission is approximately $15 for adults and $5 for children.

- *Charles Hosmer Morse Museum of American Art*: Explore a beautiful Tiffany glass collection. Adult tickets are roughly $6 and children's tickets are around $1.

- *Performing Arts Shows*: Attend local theater and ballet events such as Dr. Phillips Center for the Performing Arts, with ticket prices ranging according to the show and venue.

Food and Dining

Orlando's culinary industry has expanded dramatically in recent years, providing a wide range of dining options:

- *Food Festivals*: At food festivals such as the Epcot International Food & Wine Festival and the Orlando Food and Wine Festival, you can sample a range of cuisines. Dishes are priced differently.

- *Farm-to-Table Dining*: Enjoy farm-fresh meals at eateries such as The Ravenous Pig, where entrees start around $30.

- *International Cuisine*: Discover Orlando's rich international culinary culture, where costs range from $10 for street food to $100 or more for gourmet dining.

Nightlife

When the sun goes down, Orlando's nightlife comes to life:

- Visit popular nightlife zones such as *Church Street* and *Wall Street Plaza,* where cover charges and drink prices vary.

- *Live Music Venues*: Attend live music performances at venues such as the House of Blues or the Social. Ticket prices vary according to the artist and event.

- *Nightclubs*: Get your groove on in clubs like EVE Orlando or Tier Nightclub, where cover charges normally run from $10 to $30.

Remember that rates and availability are subject to change, so be sure to check the most recent information and plan your schedule accordingly.

Now that you have learned the fundamentals of Orlando, it is time to explore the city's heart. In the next chapters, we will look more into the city's most famous attractions, different neighborhoods, food options, and everything else that makes Orlando such a special place. So buckle up, and prepare for an incredible journey in Florida's crown jewel!

Chapter 3

Exploring the Neighborhoods of Orlando

Orlando, Florida, is a bustling and diverse city with numerous areas to discover. In this chapter, we will look at some of the most iconic and culturally rich neighborhoods in Orlando.

Downtown Orlando

Downtown Orlando is the pulsing core of the city, distinguished by its stunning skyscrapers, cultural events, and lively streets. It is a hive of activity both during the day and at night, with a mix of entertainment, food, and commerce.

Highlights

Lake Eola Overview
Lake Eola, has a gorgeous park surrounding the tranquil lake, and is located in the heart of downtown. Rent swan-shaped paddle boats so you can feed the resident swans and ducks, or simply

meander around. Concerts and other events are frequently held at the Walt Disney Amphitheater.

Cost For renting a Paddle Boat: Typically, renting a paddle boat at Lake Eola costs roughly $15 per hour.

Eola House: This old structure by the lake is frequently used for cultural events and weddings. It is a famous photography location due to its architecture and tranquil surroundings.

Relaxation: There is lots of green area in the park for picnics, sunbathing, or simply relaxing under the shadow of enormous oak trees.

Cost for visiting the Park: Visiting the park is normally free, making it a cost-effective alternative.

Dr. Phillips Center for the Performing Arts

This cutting-edge theater hosts everything from Broadway plays to ballet and concerts. Check out their calendar for upcoming events.

Ticket costs range from $30 to $150 or more depending on the performance and performers.

Dining: Downtown Orlando has a wide variety of restaurants to satisfy all tastes. There is something for everyone here, from trendy food halls like

Market on Magnolia to elegant eateries like The *Boheme*.

Dining Cost: Dining costs vary greatly, but most places charge between $20 and $50 per person.

Overview of the City Arts District

The City Arts District is a creative and cultural hotspot noted for its thriving art scene and historic buildings. It is a refuge for both artists and art fans.

Highlights

The Orlando Museum of Art features a wide collection of American, African, and modern art. It frequently has rotating exhibits, so there is always something fresh to see.

Cost: Adult admission is usually around $15, with reductions for seniors and students.

The Art Galleries

Stroll among the many art galleries that line the streets of the neighborhood. There is a vast range of art styles available, from classic to avant-garde.

Cost: While many galleries provide free access, the prices of art works vary greatly.

Thornton Park is a lovely residential neighborhood adjacent to the City Arts District with tree-lined streets, boutique stores, and superb dining options.

Overview Of The Historic Church Street District

Travel back in time and enjoy the elegance of Orlando's Historic Church Street District. This neighborhood mixes historical relevance with contemporary entertainment opportunities.

Highlights

Church Street Station is a well-known entertainment complex including restaurants, pubs, and live music venues. It is a terrific spot for a night out with friends.

Cover rates for clubs and bars vary, but are normally between $10 and $20.

Every Sunday, the Orlando Farmers Market offers fresh vegetables, handmade crafts, and gourmet meals. It is a fun way to spend a Saturday morning.

Cost: There is no charge to browse; pricing for things vary.

Historic Architecture: You can Stroll the streets and observe the district's historic architecture, which goes back to the late 1800s.

I-Drive (International Drive)

Welcome to International Drive, also known as I-Drive, the busy center of Orlando's entertainment sector. This historic boulevard runs across the city for nearly 11 miles, offering a diverse choice of attractions, food options, and retail experiences.

Here in this section, we will **Highlight** some of the must-see attractions along I-Drive, such as ICON Park, Pointe Orlando, and the numerous retail choices available in this busy region.

A more elaborate information on the ICONic Attractions in I-Drive will be given in chapter 3, this is just a highlight **:)**

The ICON Park

ICON Park is a premier entertainment facility located on International Drive's northern terminus. This multi-acre location provides a variety of dining, shopping, and entertainment opportunities for a fun-filled day or evening. Here are a few examples:

The Wheel: At the heart of ICON Park is "The Wheel," a tall observation wheel with panoramic views of the Orlando skyline. This 400-foot-tall observation wheel is one of the tallest on the East Coast.

A ride ticket normally costs between $27 to $32 for adults and $22 to $27 for youngsters, with discounts frequently available for online bookings.

Madame Tussauds Orlando: Located just a few minutes' walk from The Wheel, Madame Tussauds Orlando features stunningly lifelike wax figurines of your favorite celebrities, historical figures, and pop culture icons.

Tickets typically cost between $25 to $30 for adults and $20 to $25 for youngsters, however package tickets with The Wheel provide significant savings.

SEA LIFE Orlando Aquarium: This unique underwater experience showcases a wide variety of marine life, including sharks, rays, and brightly colored fish.

Admission costs between $25 and $30 for adults and $20 to $25 for children. Tickets purchased in conjunction with other ICON Park activities can provide exceptional value.

Dining and Shopping: ICON Park has a variety of restaurants and shops to suit a wide range of tastes and preferences. Yard House, Tin Roof, and Shake Shack offer everything from casual to sophisticated dining. Meal prices can vary greatly, with informal dining often costing between $20 and $30 per person.

Live Entertainment: The complex frequently organizes live music events and unique performances, providing guests with a lively atmosphere.

I-Drive shopping

Pointe Orlando

Pointe Orlando, located at the southern end of International Drive, is another notable entertainment and shopping complex. This bustling attraction has a variety of retail outlets, restaurants, and entertainment venues. Here are a few examples:

Shopping: Pointe Orlando has a wide range of shops, from upmarket boutiques to touristy shops. Fashion, jewelry, and specialized shops abound, making it an ideal location for shopping therapy. Clothing and accessory prices can vary greatly, but there are many options to suit all budget types.

Dining: There are a variety of dining options available at the complex, ranging from informal cafes to fine dining venues. The Capital Grille, Maggiano's Little Italy, and The Pub Orlando are also popular options.

Dining prices can range from $20 per person at informal establishments to more than $50 per person at luxury establishments.

Pointe Orlando frequently hosts live music performances and events, creating an enjoyable ambiance for tourists looking for nightlife choices.

Other I-Drive shoppings

Beyond the specific shopping complexes like Pointe Orlando, International Drive is dotted with a plethora of shopping choices, ranging from high-end boutiques to eccentric souvenir shops. Here are a few memorable shopping experiences:

Orlando International Premium shops: These shops, located on the northern end of I-Drive, provide great savings on designer and name-brand products. Clothing, accessories, footwear, and other items are frequently 25% to 65% off typical retail prices.

Souvenir stores: International Drive is packed with souvenir stores selling everything from Disney-themed souvenirs to Florida citrus-themed presents. Prices vary, but you will find reasonably priced mementos and gifts.

I-Drive 360: In addition to ICON Park, I-Drive 360 provides shopping possibilities, such as unique shops and specialty stores where you may find unusual things.

Orlando Vineland Premium Outlets: These premium outlets, located slightly off International Drive, are worth a visit if you are a serious shopper. You can get high-end apparel, electronics, and homeware at a fraction of the price.

We have looked at the rich tapestry of experiences on International Drive, from the glittering activities at ICON Park to the shopping delights of Pointe Orlando and the different shopping choices along this historic avenue.

I-Drive major ICONic Attractions would be further discussed in the next chapter. Have fun and see you there!

Chapter 4

Major Theme Parks and Attractions

Orlando, located in the heart of the Sunshine State, is well-known for its major amusement parks and attractions, which attract millions of people from all over the world each year.

Together, we will explore the beautiful world of Orlando's biggest theme parks and attractions in this travel guide, giving you a taste of the amazing entertainment, **_Thrilling Rides_**, and immersive adventures that await you.

Orlando provides a broad choice of attractions to suit any traveler's interests, from the dazzling enchantment of Walt Disney World Resort to the wizarding wonders of **_The Wizarding World of Harry Potter_** at Universal Orlando Resort.

Orlando has it all, whether you are looking for adrenaline-pumping roller coasters, engaging animal encounters, or a chance to meet your **_favorite cartoon characters_**.

Come along as we explore the key theme parks and attractions that make Orlando a renowned holiday destination. Prepare to be enchanted by the enchantment, excitement, and pure joy that only Orlando can deliver. So pack your luggage and get ready for an incredible journey at the world's theme park capital!

Walt Disney World Resort

Few destinations can compete with the pure charm and enchantment offered by the Walt Disney World Resort in Orlando, Florida, when it comes to world-class theme parks and attractions.

This huge entertainment complex, spanning over 25,000 acres, is a wonderful destination for families, adventurers, and Disney fans of all ages. This chapter delves into the core of Disney enchantment, visiting two of the company's most iconic parks: enchantment Kingdom and Epcot.

The Magic Kingdom

A Place Where Dreams Come True
Overview: The Magic Kingdom is frequently referred to as Walt Disney World Resort's crown gem. With its fairytale castle at its heart, this park is a realm of fantasy, imagination, and amazing memories.

Main Street, U.S.A., Adventureland, Frontierland, Liberty Square, Fantasyland, and Tomorrowland are the six separate lands. Each land has its own set of activities, entertainment, and culinary options.

Attractions To See

Cinderella Castle: Cinderella Castle, the park's distinctive symbol, sits tall in the park's center. Each night, the castle is illuminated by the wonderful "*Happily Ever After*" fireworks and projection show.

Pirates of the Caribbean: This legendary attraction takes you on a daring voyage across pirate-infested waters. The attraction includes robotic pirates, enthralling stories, and a catchy theme tune.

Space Mountain: This exhilarating indoor roller coaster transports you to outer space at incredible speeds. The dark, cosmic setting lends a sense of intrigue to the encounter.

The 999 Cheerful Haunts: Step inside this eerie yet lovely attraction, a haunting manor filled with the "999 cheerful haunts."

It is a fan favorite because of the combination of creepy effects and whimsical humor that would definitely give you that satisfying adrenaline rush you don't even realize that you need.

Seven Dwarfs Mine Train: A family-friendly roller coaster that provides a unique swinging mine cart ride through Snow White and the Seven Dwarfs' universe.

Special Dining: While there are numerous dining options in the Magic Kingdom, ensure to make a reservation at Cinderella's Royal Table for a magnificent dining experience within Cinderella Castle.

Depending on the lunchtime and season, prices might range from $60 to $80 per person.

Entry Ticket Prices For The Magic Kingdom
A one-day ticket to Magic Kingdom normally costs between $109 and $159 for adults (ages 10 and up) and between $103 and $153 for children (ages 3 to 9). Prices may differ depending on high seasons and special events.

Epcot World of Discovery

Overview
Epcot, which stands for Experimental Prototype Community Of Tomorrow, is a one-of-a-kind combination of futuristic innovation and worldwide adventure. Future World and World Showcase are the two primary components of this attraction.

Future World exhibits cutting-edge technology and scientific advances, whilst the World Showcase immerses visitors in the culture and cuisine of 11 various countries and much more.

Attractions You'd-See

Spaceship Earth: The distinctive geodesic sphere known as Spaceship Earth can not be missed as you enter Epcot. Inside, you will start on a trip through communication and technology history.

Soarin' The World: An incredible virtual hang glider experience that takes you on a tour of the world's most recognizable sights.

Test Track: Create your own virtual car and then race it around a high-speed track to see how it performs.

Frozen Ever After: Take a charming boat ride through the icy world of Frozen, filled with favorite songs from the film, with with special appearances from Anna, Elsa, and Olaf.

World Showcase: Take a stroll around the World Showcase Lagoon and visit the pavilions representing Canada, the United Kingdom, France, Morocco, Japan, the United States, Italy, Germany, China, Norway, and Mexico.

The 11 pavilions representing countries from across the world. Do not miss the dining, shopping, and cultural entertainment experiences that are unique to each pavilion.

Dining options

Dining options at Epcot's World Showcase range from French cuisine at Les Chefs de France to Japanese teppanyaki grills at Teppan Edo and much more. Table-service eating might cost between $40 and $70 per person.

Ticket Prices: A one-day ticket to Epcot is priced similarly to Magic Kingdom, ranging from $109 to $159 for adults and $103 to $153 for children.

The Walt Disney World Resort's Magic Kingdom and Epcot are more than just theme parks; they are immersive experiences that take guests into the worlds of classic Disney tales and global adventure. Buckle up, because Your trip through Disney's enchantment is just getting started.

Hollywood Studios at Disney

Overview

Disney's Hollywood Studios located near Bay Lake is one of four theme parks in the Walt Disney World Resort in Orlando Florida.

This theme park celebrates the enchantment of show business by immersing guests in the worlds of film, television, and entertainment.

Attractions You'd See

Star Wars Galaxy's Edge: Immerse yourself in a galaxy far, far away with attractions such as Millennium Falcon: Smugglers Run and Rise of the Resistance. Here's a tip for Star Wars aficionados, a visit to the Black Spire Outpost is a must!

Toy Story Land: Slinky Dog Dash and Toy Story Mania bring the wonder of Andy's backyard to life. Remember to take pictures with Woody and Buzz Lightyear.

Hollywood Tower Hotel
The Twilight Zone Tower of Terror :(
Immerse yourself in the scary and thrilling narrative of this haunted hotel, which offers a heart-pounding drop that's not for the faint of heart.

The price for *Single-day Tickets* to Disney's Hollywood Studios begins at around $109 for adults and $103 for youngsters aged 3-9. The prices may change depending on the season and any special offers or promotions.

Disney's Animal Kingdom

Overview

Disney's Animal Kingdom, located in Bay Lake, Florida, is another enthralling park inside the Walt Disney World Resort. It combines the wonder of the natural world with the magic of Disney, providing a unique blend of animal interactions and exhilarating attractions.

Attractions You'd-See

Pandora - The World of Avatar: Discover Pandora's bioluminescent forests with attractions such as Avatar Flight of Passage and Na'vi River Journey. The floating mountains are also breathtaking.

Kilimanjaro Safaris: Go on a true African safari journey on the kilimanjaro to see lions, giraffes, and elephants in their native habitat.

Expedition Everest: Prepare for a thrilling roller coaster ride over the Himalayas' Everest, including an harrowing encounter with the Yeti.

Ticket Prices: As of September 2021, single-day tickets to Disney's Animal Kingdom cost around $109 for adults and $103 for youngsters aged 3 to 9. Prices, like those at other Disney parks, may change depending on the season and any active promotions.

Walt Disney World Resort

The Walt Disney World Resort in Bay Lake, Florida, is a sprawling entertainment complex that comprises four main theme parks (Magic Kingdom, Epcot, Disney's Hollywood Studios, and Disney's Animal Kingdom), as well as water parks, resorts, and eating options.

It is a destination in and of itself, with infinite opportunities for pleasure and relaxation.

Other Must-See Attractions: In addition to the individual parks mentioned above, the Walt Disney World Resort offers a variety of iconic experiences, such as character meet-and-greets, fireworks displays, and dining experiences such as *Be Our Guest Restaurant* in the Magic Kingdom.

Accommodation at Walt Disney World Resort ranges from budget-friendly value resorts to opulent deluxe resorts. Prices for discount resorts can range from under $100 per night to more than $500 per night for luxurious rooms.

Disney Springs

Disney Springs, formerly known as **Downtown Disney**, is a bustling retail, dining, and entertainment complex in the heart of Walt Disney World Resort. It is the ideal place to unwind and indulge in some retail therapy after a day in the parks, or to have a fantastic meal.

Notable Locations To Visit

The World of Disney: This large store is a Disney product heaven, with everything from clothing and toys to collectibles and home décor available.

The Boathouse: Enjoy riverside meals with delicious seafood and the opportunity to ride in an amphicar on the lake.

Universal Orlando Resort

Universal Orlando Resort is a massive entertainment complex that has long fascinated visitors of all ages. This huge resort includes two primary theme parks, **Universal Studios Florida** and **Universal's Islands of Adventure**, which has top attractions such as water parks, Volcano Bay, and a busy entertainment food center, and CityWalk.

The Universal Studios Florida

Universal Studios Florida is a moviegoer's fantasy come to life. You can enter into the worlds of your favorite movies and TV series right here and even be your favorite character **;-)**

Among The Most Popular Attractions Are...

The Wizarding World of Harry Potter

A trip to Universal Orlando Resort would not be complete without exploring the Wizarding World of Harry Potter. This delightful addition to the parks transports visitors into the world of J.K. Rowling's popular novel. Here are some must-see sights:

Harry Potter and the Prisoner of Azkaban: This cutting-edge attraction transports you deep into the wizarding world, where you will battle dragons and trolls beneath the legendary Gringotts bank.

Ollivanders Wand Shop: Witness an unforgettable wand-selection experience, and perhaps even have a wand choose you! (Approximate price: Wands for sale begin at $49.95.)

Buckbeak the Hippogriff: a mystical creature from the Harry Potter universe, will take you on a peaceful journey in Flight of the Hippogriff. (Estimated cost: Included with park admission)

Butterbeer: Enjoy the legendary wizarding beverage, Butterbeer, which comes in chilled, frozen, and hot varieties. (Price range: $6.99 - $7.99 depending on size and type)

Hogsmeade: Visit renowned locations such as Hogwarts Castle and the Three Broomsticks of Hogsmeade.

Attractions And Thrill Rides

Universal Orlando Resort is recognized for its adrenaline-pumping thrill coasters that cater to adrenaline junkies and thrill-seekers, such as:

The Incredible Hulk Coaster

If you are looking for an adrenaline rush, go no farther than The Incredible Hulk Coaster. You'd Feel the rush of gamma radiation as you shoot through the high-speed roller on the Incredible Hulk Coaster

This high-speed roller coaster takes you from 0 to 40 mph in less than two seconds and takes you on a crazy ride filled with loops and twists. Access to the thrill costs around $70.

Jurassic Park River excursion: The Jurassic Park River Adventure is a must-see for a more family friendly excursion. This water-based rollercoaster transports you to the prehistoric world of dinosaurs, culminating in a spectacular plummet. Watch out for the T. Rex while you are taking a boat ride around the Jurassic Park river!

Transformers-The 3D Ride: With this cutting-edge 3D ride, you can immerse yourself in the universe of Autobots and Decepticons. The $60 experience provides a thrilling narrative experience that mixes 3D images, motion simulation, and practical effects. In this realistic 3D experience, you can join the Autobots in an epic battle against the Decepticons.

The Despicable-Me Minion Chaos:
This 4D motion-simulator ride transports you into the world of Gru and his Minions, making it ideal for families. The experience costs around $50 and is a pleasant, enjoyable journey ideal for people of all ages.

The Simpsons Ride: In this funny simulator ride, you will go on a wild ride through Springfield with Homer, Marge, Bart, Lisa, and Maggie. (Estimated cost: Included with park admission)

Harry Potter and the Forbidden Journey
You will have a great time flying above the Hogwarts Castle and to meet mystical creatures in this innovative experience.

Fast and Furious -Supercharged: Join the Fast and Furious family for a high-octane adventure that blurs the barriers between film and reality. (Estimated cost: Included with park admission)

Skull Island - Reign of Kong: Take a 3D trip through the mysterious and treacherous Skull Island.

While the aforementioned costs are estimates and subject to change, Universal Orlando Resort offers a variety of ticket choices, including single-day tickets, multi-day tickets, and park-to-park passes.

Furthermore, they frequently run specials and package deals that can bring significant savings, so it is critical to check their official website for the most recent offerings.

SeaWorld Orlando

SeaWorld Orlando is a famed marine-themed park that has been enthralling visitors since its debut. It offers a balanced blend of entertainment, education, and awe-inspiring animal interactions.

Here's a comprehensive exploration of the gems that SeaWorld Orlando holds:

SeaWorld Theme Park

The SeaWorld's Theme Park Entertainment Shows

SeaWorld's live shows are the heart of its entertainment. These amazing shows feature majestic aquatic animals, including dolphins, sea lions, and the legendary killer whales, orcas.

The **"One Ocean"** show starring *Shamu*, an enormous *killer whale*, is a highlight attraction. Additionally, **"Dolphin Days"** and **"Pets Ahoy!"** gives a healthy family entertainment.

Approximate Show Admission: These fascinating shows are included with the park admission charge, which normally ranges from $80 to $110 per adult and $75 to $105 per child (ages 3-9), depending on circumstances such as the season and special promotions.

Animal Exhibits

SeaWorld Orlando boasts a broad assortment of marine life exhibits. Visitors can immerse themselves in the magical world of penguins at **"Antarctica: Empire of the Penguin"** or delve into the depths of the ocean with the **"Shark Encounter."**

Exhilarating Rides and ***Thrill Attractions*** include **"Mako"** (a hypercoaster), **"Kraken Unleashed"** (a virtual reality coaster), and **"Infinity Falls"** (a wild river rapids adventure).

Approximate Ride Admission: The cost of riding these exhilarating rides is covered by the park admission ticket.

Culinary Scene: SeaWorld has a comprehensive selection of culinary alternatives, appealing to varied tastes and interests. Visitors can eat wonderful seafood at ***"Sharks Underwater Grill"*** or grab quick, scrumptious snacks at the park's various food kiosks.

Approximate Dining Costs: Dining costs might vary but normally range from $10 to $20 per person, depending on the choice of restaurant and cuisine.

Discovery Cove

Adjacent to SeaWorld Orlando, Discovery Cove offers a unique, intimate, and engaging encounter with marine life that sets it apart from other amusement parks.
At Discovery Cove, you can;

Swim with Dolphins.

The centerpiece of Discovery Cove is the rare opportunity to swim with dolphins. Guests can build a strong connection with these extraordinary creatures, having a once-in-a-lifetime swim with them.
Dolphin Swim Experience Prices: Prices for this unique experience normally start around $200 to $250 per person and include all-day entrance to Discovery Cove.

Snorkeling

The park also has a beautiful tropical reef where tourists may snorkel with a variety of colorful fish and graceful rays.
Snorkeling fee is included in the cost of park admission.

The All-Inclusive

The all-inclusive character of Discovery Cove distinguishes it. Unlike many other parks, the admission ticket includes all meals, snacks, and beverages.

In addition, guests can take advantage of a complimentary photo package as well as the use of snorkeling equipment and wet suits.

Approximate Price For All-Inclusive Admission: Prices for this all-inclusive experience range from $200 to $350 per person, depending on factors such as the season and any continuing special deals.

Aquatica Theme Park

Aquatica, another jewel in the SeaWorld Parks & Entertainment family, is a water park that offers a refreshing mix of family fun and adventurous thrills.

Aquatica Theme Park has the following attractions you can look forward to:

Water Slides and Attractions: Aquatica features a thrilling array of water slides, including the exhilarating "Dolphin Plunge," which allows you to slide through a clear tube and get an up-close look at dolphins swimming nearby.

Admission fee: Depending on the day and current promotions, tickets to Aquatica normally vary from $60 to $90 per adult and $55 to $85 per child.

Aquatica offers a **relaxing lazy river and a sandy beach** where guests can unwind and soak up the sun; that is, for those looking for a more laid-back experience.

Aquatica Dining options: Aquatica offers a wide range of dining alternatives, from quick-service restaurants to full-service restaurants. There is something for everyone's taste, whether it be burgers or seafood.

Dining fees at Aquatica normally range between $10 and $20 per person, depending on the restaurant and menu selection.

SeaWorld Orlando, Discovery Cove, and Aquatica Water Park provide a diverse range of experiences for guests of all ages. These attractions have something for everyone, whether you are looking for heart-pounding thrills, intimate animal interactions, or simply a day of relaxation.

Note: That *when planning your trip, be sure to check the most up-to-date pricing and availability, since they can change according on the time of year and any ongoing special specials.*

LEGOLAND Florida Resort

When it comes to big theme parks and attractions, the word LEGOLAND Florida Resort immediately catches the attention of both children and adults.

This landmark location exemplifies the enduring popularity of the beloved LEGO brand, which is known for inspiring creativity and providing many hours of entertainment.

Here we will look at the two main attractions at LEGOLAND Florida Resort: the LEGOLAND Theme Park and the LEGOLAND Water Park.

LEGOLAND Theme Park

The LEGOLAND Theme Park at LEGOLAND Florida Resort is a huge creative and adventure playground.

This park is designed for families with children aged 2 to 12, and it has a variety of attractions that cater to a wide range of interests and tastes.

The general park admission fee ranges from $90 to $110 per person. Here are the top picks for LEGOLAND Theme Park:

Miniland USA

Miniland USA is one of the most intriguing elements of LEGOLAND Florida Resort. It is an elaborate model village with famous American landmarks and cityscapes that have been expertly constructed using LEGO bricks.

This attraction is a wonder of engineering and innovation, stretching from the Statue of Liberty to the Kennedy Space Center.

The World Of LEGO NINJAGO

Enter the fascinating world of **LEGO NINJAGO**, where you may use ninja skills and interactive technology to fight evil forces.

The immersive attraction blends physical obstacles with digital activity and is popular with both children and adults.

Coastersaurus

This family-friendly roller coaster provides an exciting yet approachable ride for younger riders. The coaster transports you to a prehistoric LEGO world populated by life-sized LEGO brick dinosaurs.

LEGO City

At LEGO City, kids may go on real-life activities like piloting their own boats, fighting fires, and driving

LEGO cars. It is a fun and informative area that stimulates imaginative play.

The Dragon

For those looking for a more thrilling ride, The Dragon is a roller coaster that takes you through a medieval LEGO castle complete with animated LEGO monsters.

LEGOLAND Florida Hotel

While not strictly a theme park, the LEGOLAND Florida Hotel is located on the resort grounds and offers LEGO-themed rooms, character meet-and-greets, and easy access to the park.

Room costs normally range between $150 and $200 per night.

LEGOLAND Water Park

The LEGOLAND Water Park, located adjacent to the LEGOLAND Theme Park and offers a cool respite from the Florida heat. This water park has been constructed with the same care and inventiveness as its counterpart.

Build-A-Raft River

Visitors may build their own custom LEGO rafts and float down a lazy river filled with fun LEGO-themed attractions.

Admission is included with the Water Park upgrade, which may be added to your LEGOLAND Theme Park ticket for $30 to $40 per person.

Splash Out

Splash Out, a trio of body slides that plunge riders into a refreshing pool, will appeal to thrill seekers. Each slide provides a distinct level of thrill, making it appropriate for people of all ages.

Joker Soaker

This interactive playground includes a variety of water cannons as well as a big bucket that periodically drops gallons of water on unsuspecting visitors.

Wave Pool

Unwind in the wave pool, where gentle waves make swimming and cooling off pleasant and safe.

Beach Retreat

The LEGOLAND Beach Retreat, like the LEGOLAND Florida Hotel, provides lodging near the Water Park. Each villa is furnished with LEGO theming and offers a relaxing coastal setting.

Pricing: Bungalow costs normally range between $200 and $250 per night.

Kennedy Space Center Visitor Complex

Introduction

The Kennedy Space Center (KSC) Visitor Complex is located on Florida's picturesque Space Coast and it's a must-visit destination for anyone interested in space exploration, science, and history.

This iconic attraction offers an immersive experience that takes visitors on a journey through America's incredible space program. Here's what you can expect when you visit the Kennedy Space Center Visitor Complex:

Rocket Garden

At the Rocket Garden, you can marvel at the outdoor display featuring real rockets from various missions to space. Explore the Mercury-Redstone, Gemini-Titan, and Saturn 1B rockets that played pivotal roles in NASA's early space programs. It's an excellent photo opportunity for space enthusiasts.

Space Shuttle Atlantis

Get up close and personal with the Space Shuttle Atlantis, one of NASA's most iconic spacecraft. The Atlantis exhibit allows visitors to see the shuttle in all its glory, complete with a full-scale replica of the Hubble Space Telescope.

Interactive displays and multimedia presentations provide insights into the shuttle's missions and the astronauts who flew aboard.

Shuttle Launch Experience

Strap in and prepare for liftoff as you experience the Shuttle Launch Experience simulator. This thrilling attraction lets you feel the intense vibrations and G-forces of a shuttle launch. It's the closest most of us will ever get to experiencing space travel.

Astronaut Encounter

Meet a real astronaut and hear first hand stories about life in space during the Astronaut Encounter program. You'll have the chance to have an out-of-this-world meal by dining with an astronaut, to ask questions, take photos, and gain unique insights into the challenges and rewards of space exploration.

The IMAX Theater

Watch awe-inspiring space films in the IMAX Theater, featuring a massive five-story screen and state-of-the-art sound. These films offer a close-up look at missions to the International Space Station and the mysteries of the cosmos.

Rocket Launch Viewing

Check the schedule for upcoming rocket launches from Kennedy Space Center. If you're lucky, you might be able to witness a live launch. Viewing locations vary depending on the launch, but each offers a spectacular view of the rocket ascending into space.

Space Center Bus Tour

Hop aboard a guided bus tour that takes you behind the scenes at Kennedy Space Center. Visit launch pads, the *Vehicle Assembly Building* (one of the largest buildings in the world), and the Launch Control Center.

The tour provides a deeper understanding of NASA's operations as well as the preparation of spacecraft for launch.

Educational Opportunities

For those seeking a deeper understanding of space and space exploration, the Kennedy Space Center Visitor Complex offers educational opportunities that go beyond the standard visitor experience.

Here you can learn about the educational programs and resources available at KSC, making it an excellent destination for students and aspiring scientists. These include:

KSC Up-Close Tours - These guided tours take visitors behind the scenes at KSC, offering a close-up look at launch pads, control centers, and facilities not typically accessible to the public.

Camp KSC - Camp KSC is an immersive, multi-day camp experience for children and families. Participants can engage in hands-on STEM activities, meet astronauts, and explore the complex in a unique way.

STEM Learning - The Kennedy Space Center is committed to promoting STEM (Science, Technology, Engineering, and Mathematics) education. Numerous interactive exhibits and programs are designed to inspire the next generation of scientists and engineers.

Practical Information

Location: Kennedy Space Center Visitor Complex is located on Merritt Island, Florida, just east of Orlando.

Operating Hours: The complex's hours of operation may vary, so it's advisable to check the official website for current information before planning your visit.

Tickets: Admission prices vary depending on age and the type of experience you choose. Discounts are often available for children, seniors, and veterans.

Accessibility: The complex is wheelchair accessible, and accommodations can be made for visitors with disabilities.

Dining and Souvenirs

The complex offers several dining options and gift shops where you can purchase space-themed souvenirs.

Dining

Orbit Café

Enjoy a variety of dining options, including space-themed dishes, at the Orbit Café. Fuel up for your adventure with astronaut-approved cuisine.

Rocket Garden Café

Enjoy a meal or snack at the Rocket Garden Café, where you can dine surrounded by historic rockets. The café offers a range of options to satisfy your hunger as you continue your journey through the complex.

Space Shopping And Souvenirs

Browse a wide selection of space-themed souvenirs, apparel, and memorabilia, so you can take home a piece of space history as a lasting memento of your visit.

Discover the perfect keepsakes to commemorate your visit to KSC. Explore the Space Shop's vast selection of space-themed merchandise, from astronaut ice cream to mission patches.

You can also find a wide range of space-themed souvenirs, including clothing, toys, books, and astronaut ice creams here.

I-Drive ICONic Attractions

Madame Tussauds Orlando

... A Surreal Close Encounter with the Stars
Madame Tussauds is a wax museum. Orlando is a spectacular wax museum that allows visitors to interact with some of the world's most renowned celebrities and historical people.

This attraction is part of the larger ICON Park complex, which is a hub for entertainment and dining and is located in the middle of Orlando's bustling entertainment sector.

Madame Tussauds features amazingly lifelike wax figurines of celebrities such as Beyoncé, Leonardo DiCaprio, Albert Einstein, and even popular Disney characters such as Mickey Mouse.

The experience here is more than just looking at these incredible wax figurines; it is also interactive. You can pose for photos with your favorite celebs and even attend themed events and parties.

Consider snapping a selfie with Spider-Man or dancing with Taylor Swift within the limits of this enthralling attraction. Tickets are normally priced between $20 and $30 per person, with discounts available for children and seniors.

The Wheel at ICON Park

...Soaring New Heights

The Wheel at ICON Park, which is adjacent to Madame Tussauds Orlando, is another renowned landmark that dominates the Orlando skyline.

This huge observation wheel provides panoramic views of the city and its neighboring attractions. It is one of the tallest observation wheels in the United States, standing 400 feet tall.

A ride on The Wheel is an unforgettable experience. Each of the 30 air-conditioned capsules has a touchscreen tablet with information on the landmarks you are seeing.

Whether you visit during the day to see the sweeping metropolis or at night to see the shimmering lights of Orlando, this site will leave you speechless. A ride on The Wheel normally costs between $20 and $30 for adults, with lower pricing for youngsters.

Ripley's Believe It or Not!

...Odditiesz Galore!

If you have a taste for the strange and unexpected, Ripley's Believe It or Not! in Orlando is the place to go. This attraction, located on International Drive, is part of the Ripley's business, which is recognized for its collection of oddities, curiosities, and fantastic relics.

Inside Ripley's Believe It or Not!, you will find a diverse collection of exhibitions that push the boundaries of what you thought was possible.

From shrunken heads and eccentric art pieces to optical illusions that will leave your mind spinning, this site is a haven for those who enjoy the strange and unusual. Adult entry fees normally vary from $15 to $25, with discounts available for children and seniors.

Kissimmee And Beyond

Kissimmee and the surrounding Central Florida areas are hard to top when it comes to world-class entertainment and family-friendly attractions.

This section will take you on an exciting journey around some of Kissimmee's most popular theme parks and attractions, highlighting the varied range of activities offered to visitors of all ages.

Kissimmee's Historic District

Old Town, located in the heart of Kissimmee, is a nostalgic excursion back in time. This beautiful site combines history and current entertainment in a unique way, making it a must-see for anybody visiting the area.

The cobblestone lanes of Old Town are lined with quaint shops, restaurants, and classic car displays that transport you to another era.

Kissimmee's Key Features
Saturday Night Car Excursions
Old Town is well-known for its Friday and Saturday night car excursions. The streets are lined with classic and custom cars from various eras, providing a visual spectacle that automotive aficionados will enjoy.

Shopping

Take a stroll around the quaint boutiques and shops, where you can discover everything from vintage clothing to one-of-a-kind gifts. Prices vary, but you may expect to get both low-cost and high-end items.

Amusement Rides
There are several family-friendly amusement rides in Old Town, including a Ferris wheel and a classic carousel. Individual rides cost between $3 and $6 per person, with all-day riding wristbands costing roughly $15.

Live entertainment is available on the Old Town stage, including music performers and magic shows. Specific events and costs may differ depending on the program.

Gatorland

Gatorland, a short drive from Kissimmee, is a popular Florida attraction that offers up-close encounters with the state's most famous reptile residents: alligators. Gatorland is a family-friendly excursion with over 100 acres of swamps, exhibitions, and wildlife encounters.

Key Features
Take a ride on the Gatorland Express Train to tour the park and get up close and personal with alligators, birds, and other native animals. Tickets cost about $3 per person.

Professional *"Gator Wrestlers"* do risky acts and teach people about these wonderful creatures in gator wrestling shows. Show admission is included with park admission.

Screamin' Gator Zip Line

Fly above the alligator breeding marsh on the Screamin' Gator Zip Line for an adrenaline sensation. Prices begin around $70 per person.

Up-Close Encounters

Gatorland provides guests with unique experiences such as the Trainer-for-a-Day program and the Adventure Hour, which let them to interact with and learn about alligators and other creatures. Prices vary according to the program selected.

Wildlife and Nature Preserves

The natural splendor of Central Florida stretches far beyond its tourist parks. There are various wildlife and environment preserves in the area that provide a calm respite from the rush and bustle of the attractions.

Here are a few interesting alternatives:

Shingle Creek Regional Park

Located in Kissimmee, this park has hiking and bike paths, picnic sites, and opportunities for birdwatching along the gorgeous Shingle Creek. Typically, admission is free.

Lake Tohopekaliga (Lake Toho)

This massive lake, sometimes known as Toho for short, is a popular destination for fishing, boating, and birdwatching. A kayak or pontoon boat can be rented for $25 to $60 per hour, depending on the size of the craft.

Tibet-Butler Nature Preserve

This preserve, located near Orlando, offers hiking routes through lush forests and wetlands. Because admission is free, it is an excellent value for nature lovers.

Chapter 5

Outdoor Adventures

Central Florida Parks

Nature lovers and thrill seekers are in for a treat in Central Florida. The region is home to a wealth of outdoor places, each with its own distinct charm and recreational activities.

We will look at three must-see outdoor places in this chapter: Wekiwa Springs State Park, Blue Spring State Park, and The Ocala National Forest.

Wekiwa Springs State Park

... A Natural Oasis

Wekiwa Springs State Park, located just 20 minutes north of Orlando, entices visitors with its unspoilt beauty of pure waters. This outdoor refuge is an exquisite getaway where the noise of modern life gives way to nature's tranquility.

Wekiwa Springs, located in the center of the park, is a crystalline spring with water so beautiful that it appears almost dreamlike.

The Beautiful Waters

Wekiwa Springs is without a doubt the crown treasure of this state park. The spring is fed by a natural underground aquifer, and maintains a consistent temperature of 72 degrees Fahrenheit all year.

The water is so clear that you can see the limestone floor, producing a stunning turquoise pool that beckons visitors to take a refreshing dip. Wekiwa Springs' welcoming waters are a natural retreat, whenever you wish to escape the searing Florida heat or simply connect with nature.

Activities for Everyone

Wekiwa Springs State Park has a wide variety of activities for visitors of all ages and interests, including:

Swimming: Wekiwa Springs' swimming area is a highlight of the park. Its sandy bottom and rich, subtropical vegetation make it an enchanting backdrop for a leisurely swim. The steady spring water temperature makes the experience delightful all year.

Canoeing and kayaking

You can rent a canoe or kayak and take a peaceful voyage along the Wekiva River, which has been designated as a National Wild and Scenic River.

Paddling across the meandering canals, you will come upon a vibrant environment, complete with turtles, birds, and possibly even an alligator.

Hiking

Wekiwa Springs has a number of hiking paths that wind through a variety of environments. The Sand Lake Trail, for example, brings you through pine flatwoods, allowing you to see Florida's unique flora and fauna.

Camping

For those who want to stay longer, the park has a campground with space for both RVs and tents. Camping under the Florida night sky allows you to totally immerse yourself in the natural ambiance.

Picnicking

There are several attractive picnic spots with grills throughout the park. It is a great place to get together with family and friends for a BBQ while enjoying the peace and quiet of the natural surroundings.

The admission fee for Wekiwa Springs State Park is approximately $6 per vehicle. However, pricing *may have changed, so check the current rates before arranging your trip.*

Wekiwa Springs State Park is a haven where the contemporary world fades away, leaving only nature's sights and sounds that'll bring you connectivity and aid you in finding tranquility.

Whenever you are looking for adventure, relaxation, or a little of both, this Central Florida treasure delivers an amazing experience that will leave you fascinated by Sunshine State's magnificence.

Blue Spring State Park

...A Relaxing Haven for Manatees and Nature Lovers

Blue Spring State Park, located in the heart of Central Florida near the lovely town of Orange City, is a natural wonderland that appeals to both animal aficionados and outdoor explorers.

This 2,600-acre park is notable for its crystal-clear spring, which maintains at a consistent and welcoming 72 degrees Fahrenheit all year. While Blue Spring State Park has a range of activities, its claim to fame is that it is a winter haven for West Indian manatees.

The Manatee Sanctuary

Blue Spring is transformed into a warm and safe home for West Indian manatees throughout the winter season, which lasts from November to March.

As the air temperature lowers, these marine creatures seek shelter in the warm waters of spring. Seeing manatees is probably one of the park's most popular activities during this time of year.

Visitors congregate along elevated boardwalks that provide good vantage points for viewing these gorgeous creatures in their native habitat. The sight of manatees effortlessly swimming through the crystal-clear seas is nothing short of beautiful, and it makes for great photo possibilities.

Springtime Swimming

While manatee season restricts swimming in Blue Spring to preserve the manatees, the spring reopens to swimming lovers once the warmer months begin.

With its sandy bottom and attractive turquoise waters, the spring basin is an ideal site for a relaxing swim. It stands in stark contrast to the chillier, spring-run swimming pools seen in other Florida parks, making it a favorite summer destination for visitors wishing to cool off.

Kayaking and canoeing

Blue Spring exploration extends beyond the spring basin. Canoeing and kayaking are available along the tranquil St. Johns River in the park.

You may rent a canoe or kayak and paddle across this scenic stream, where you may see river otters, alligators, and other bird species. Paddling is a calm way to connect with nature and immerse yourself in the quiet surroundings.

Trails for Hiking

Blue Spring State Park has various well-maintained hiking paths that weave through its diverse ecosystems for those who want to stay on dry land. These trails range in length from short, family-friendly loops to longer, more difficult treks.

Keep a watch out for local animals including white-tailed deer, gopher tortoises, and a variety of bird species as you wander through the pine flatwoods and hardwood hammocks. The 1.8-mile Pine Island Trail is a wonderful introduction to the park's natural beauty.

Camping In The Wilderness

Blue Spring State Park has a campground with spots for both tent and RV campers for those who want to stay longer. The campgrounds provide a tranquil and attractive location surrounded by nature's noises.

A fantastic camping trip includes campfires, starry skies, and the relaxing sounds of the St. Johns River.

Admission Fee

The admission fee for Blue Spring State Park was $6 per vehicle. There were also different costs for boat tours and rentals. To guarantee you have the most up-to-date information, confirm the current fees and any changes before organizing your visit.

Ocala National Forest

...Florida's Untamed Wilderness

Ocala National Forest, located in the heart of Central Florida, is a monument to the Sunshine State's untamed splendor.

This vast natural beauty, spanning over 600 square miles, is the continental United States' southernmost national forest. Its various habitats and wide range of outdoor activities make it a must-see for those looking for a true wilderness experience.

A Handmade Tapestry

Ocala National Forest is a fascinating mix of ecosystems, each with its own distinct personality. You will come across towering longleaf pine woods, virgin cypress swamps, meandering blackwater rivers, and dazzling lakes as you travel over its immense expanse. This diversified terrain serves as the backdrop for a variety of outdoor activities.

Backpacking and hiking

Ocala National Forest is a hiking and backpacking paradise just waiting to be discovered. The Florida National Scenic Trail, which covers over 1,000 miles through the state and offers an immersive journey through Florida's various landscapes, is the crown jewel of hiking adventures here.

There are numerous pathways within the forest that appeal to different ability levels, from leisurely strolls through **pine-scented _woodlands_** to strenuous treks along the banks of **_tranquil lakes_**.

Be prepared to encounter the delights of Florida's flora and fauna as you travel these paths, from the colorful blooming of _wildflowers to the stealthy movements of wildlife._

Equestrians who enjoy horseback riding will love Ocala National Forest. The forest has a network of horse-friendly pathways that allow riders to explore the area on horseback.

These marked routes wind through magnificent woodlands and provide stunning views along the way. There are also horse campsites where riders can rest, relax, and bond with their equine companions beneath the night sky of Florida.

Water aficionados who enjoy fishing and boating are also in for a treat. The forest is home to a plethora of lakes, rivers, and springs teeming with aquatic life. Lake George, one of Florida's largest lakes, entices fishermen with the promise of great fishing.

Camping in the Backcountry

Camping is a must-do activity when visiting the Ocala National Forest. The woodland has a variety of camping choices to suit any camper's preferences.

There are rustic camping sites nestled away in isolated sections of the forest where you may fully unplug from the modern world if you are looking for a true wilderness immersion.

Alternatively, constructed campgrounds with amenities such as restrooms, picnic tables, and fire rings are available for those who like some creature comforts.

Camping in this rich environment allows you to hear the nighttime chorus of crickets, smell the perfume of pine, and stare at a star-studded night sky.

Off-Roading Excursions

Ocala National Forest has dedicated off-road trails for thrill seekers and off-road enthusiasts. The

Ocala North OHV Trail System is a popular option, offering ATV and OHV riders an exciting experience.

These routes wind through the steep terrain of the forest, providing a hard and exhilarating trip for those who enjoy the extreme.

Ocala National Forest entices individuals seeking adventure by providing a symphony of natural beauty and excitement.

This untamed wilderness delivers memorable experiences and cherished memories in the midst of Florida's gorgeous sceneries, whether you are a hiker, camper, equestrian, angler, or off-road enthusiast.

Remember to check the most up-to-date information before venturing into this natural wonderland.

Airboat Tours In The Everglades

The Florida Everglades, located just outside of Orlando, provide a once-in-a-lifetime opportunity to explore one of North America's most diverse ecosystems. Airboat trips are a popular method to get close to this incredible countryside.

What You Can Expect

Airboat tours are normally led by expert operators who will take you through the Everglades' twisting canals. Large propellers at the back of these boats enable for smooth, shallow-water cruising.

Highlights Of The Everglades

Wildlife Encounters: Keep a watch out for alligators, turtles, numerous bird species, and, if you are lucky, manatees.

Views: Take in the natural splendor of the Everglades, including its rich vegetation and distinctive sceneries.

Knowledgeable guides will give insights about the ecology, its history, and the importance of conservation.

Price Estimates

Standard Airboat Tour: $25 - $50 (duration: 1-2 hours)

Private airboat tours are from $200 to $500 per boat (time varies depending on group size).

Combo Tours: Some tour companies offer package deals that incorporate animal encounters or other activities. Prices differ.

Operators Recommendations

Wild Florida Airboats & Gator Park: This attraction is well-known for its wildlife encounters and informative tours.

Boggy Creek Airboat Adventures Provides night tours for a one-of-a-kind experience.

Hot Air Ballooning

Fly above Orlando in a hot air balloon for a genuinely amazing experience. This tranquil excursion offers spectacular panoramic views of Central Florida.

What You Can Expect
Hot air ballooning is a calm and serene method to explore the varied terrain of the region. You will soar into the skies, enjoying the pleasant breeze and taking in the sights below.

Highlights
Sunrise Serenity: The majority of hot air balloon trips are arranged at sunrise, when the sky are clear and the lighting is ideal for photography.

View from Above: Take in breathtaking views of Orlando's theme parks, lakes, and lush foliage.

Champagne Toast: To add a touch of luxury to your excursion, several operators complete the journey with a champagne toast.

Price Estimates

A **standard hot air balloon ride** costs between $175 and $250 per person (duration: 1 hour).

Private Balloon Rides: From $1,000 to $1,500 for a private flight for two or more persons (duration: 1-1.5 hours).

Operators Recommendations

Orlando Balloon Rides: Shared and individual flights with competent pilots are available.

Bob's Balloon Rides is well-known for their pleasant personnel and stunning vistas.

Kayaking and Canoeing Expeditions

Kayaking and canoeing experiences in and around Orlando give an opportunity to explore quiet waterways and see local animals for those who prefer a more hands-on and interactive experience.

What You Can Expect

You can go on guided trips or rent equipment to go on your own adventure. Paddling along the waterways helps you to connect with nature more deeply.

Highlights

Wekiva River: Take a relaxing paddle down the spring-fed Wekiva River, which is known for its clean waters and green environs.

Bioluminescent Kayaking: Take a night kayaking excursion in the Indian River Lagoon to see the strange glow of bioluminescent plankton.

Wildlife Observation: See manatees, dolphins, birds, and other animals in their natural habitat.

Price Estimates

Kayak or canoe **Rentals** range from $15 to $40 per hour.

Kayaking Group Tours with a Guide $40 - $100 (length varies)
Per Person Tours are around $40 - $60 (duration: 2-3 hours).

Operators Recommendations

Wekiva Island: Kayak and canoe rentals are available, as well as guided tours.

A Day Away Kayak adventures is well-known for their bioluminescent adventures and environmentally responsible operations.

Golfin' Orlando

Orlando, Florida, is well-known for its world-class tourist parks and activities, but it is also a golfer's dream.

Orlando offers a superb golfing experience for players of all skill levels, with its lush green fairways, lovely year-round weather, and a plethora of golf courses created by some of the sport's biggest names.

In this section, we will look at the Orlando golf scene, including some of the greatest courses, estimated rates, and what to anticipate when you tee off in this sunny city.

Bay Hill Club & Lodge Golf Course

The Designed By Arnold Palmer.
@ 9000 Bay Hill Boulevard, Orlando, FL 32819

Bay Hill Club & Lodge is possibly Orlando's most well-known golf course, thanks in large part to its association with the iconic Arnold Palmer.

This 27-hole championship course provides golfers with a demanding but rewarding experience. Every year, the Arnold Palmer Invitational is held at the club, bringing some of the sport's top personalities.

A round of golf normally costs between $150 and $250, depending on the season.

TPC Sawgrass

Designed by Pete Dye
@ 5389 Great Harbor Way, Orlando, FL 32837.
TPC Sawgrass, the site of THE PLAYERS Championship, is a beautiful golf course in Orlando. This course, known for its renowned 17th hole, is both hard and visually pleasing. Prices vary, but usually begin around $175 per round.

Grand Cypress Golf Club

Designed By Jack Nicklaus
@ 1 N. Jacaranda St., Orlando, FL 32836
Jack Nicklaus built Grand Cypress Golf Club's 45-hole championship course. This club offers a great golfing experience thanks to its well manicured greens. Depending on the course and time of day, prices range from $80 to $200.

Orange County National Golf Center

Winter Garden, FL 34787, 16301 Phil Ritson Way
Panther Lake and Crooked Cat are the two championship courses at this golf complex.

The PGA Tour Q-School is held at Orange County National. Prices are lower in this area, with rates often ranging from $60 to $150.

Tee Times and Golf Packages

Consider purchasing golf packages from local resorts or golf clubs to make the most of your Orlando golfing experience. These packages frequently include lodging and playing times at prestigious golf courses.

Booking ahead of time is recommended, especially during the high season from November to April. Check the golf course's dress code, as most have severe attire requirements.

Rental of Golf Equipments

Do not worry if you forgot to bring your golf clubs! Most golf courses in Orlando have club rentals, allowing you to play a round without having to haul your equipment around. Rental fees vary, but a set of clubs will cost you between $40 and $60.

Golf Coaching

Whether you are a seasoned golfer trying to improve your game or a newbie looking to master the fundamentals, Orlando has a variety of golf teaching alternatives.

Many golf courses have PGA experts on staff who can teach you how to play. Lessons typically cost $50 to $150 per hour, depending on the instructor's experience and the facility.

Golf Tournaments

If you enjoy golf, try booking your trip around one of Orlando's golf events. Aside from the Arnold Palmer Invitational, Orlando sponsors a number of amateur and professional tournaments throughout the year.

These events are not only a terrific way to see top-tier golf, but also to immerse yourself in the local golfing culture.

For many visitors who connect Orlando exclusively with theme parks, the city's golfing culture is a well-kept secret. However, for golfers, Orlando has a varied choice of courses constructed by golf luminaries.

Orlando provides something for every golfer, from tough championship layouts to more affordable options. So, pack your clubs, make your tee appointments, and prepare to enjoy golf in the Sunshine State!

Segway Tours And Biking Trails

Orlando's natural beauty and nice weather all year round make it a great destination for outdoor enthusiasts. Whether you like exploring on two wheels or gliding easily on a Segway, Orlando has a wide range of activities for people wishing to enjoy these great outdoors.

West Orange Trail Trails for Biking
Starts at 455 E. Plant St. and ends at the Winter Garden, FL 34787.

The West Orange Trail is a 22-mile-long paved path that winds through picturesque scenery such as orange plantations and beautiful woodlands. It is ideal for bikers of all skill levels, from beginners to seasoned riders. Bikes can be rented nearby or brought with you. A full day rental normally costs between $20 and $30.

Little Econ Greenway Trail
Location: Blanchard Park, 2451 N Dean Rd, Orlando, FL 32817.
This 7-mile stretch of calm biking runs alongside the Little Econlockhatchee River. Rentals are available near the trailhead, with prices comparable to the West Orange Trail.

Cady Way Trail
Starts at Lake Baldwin Park, 2000 S Lakemont Ave, Winter Park, FL 32789.
Cady Way Trail connects Orlando with Winter Park and is 7.2 miles long. The walkway is well-kept, and rentals are available at several points along the track. Prices are relatively reasonable, ranging between $10 and $20 per hour.

Tours With Segways
Consider taking a Segway tour if you are searching for a new way to discover Orlando. These guided tours are a fun and easy way to experience the sites of the city.

i2 Segway Tours

Located at 430 N Orange Blossom Trail in Orlando, FL.

i2 Segway Tours provides a variety of guided Segway tours, including those that visit downtown Orlando, historic districts, and even at night. Prices start about $50 per person, depending on the length of the tour.

Glides of Central Florida

441 E. Central Blvd., Orlando, FL 32801

Segway excursions are available from Central Florida Glides around Lake Eola and downtown Orlando. The knowledgeable tour guides provide information on the city's history and attractions. Tours usually run 1 to 2 hours and cost between $50 and $75 per person.

There is no shortage of outdoor adventure in Orlando, for persons who like the freedom of exploring Orlando's stunning surroundings on a bike or the unique sensation of gliding across the city on a Segway and much more.

The city's bicycle trails and Segway excursions provide a pleasant and immersive opportunity to connect with this Florida treasure's natural beauty and colorful culture. So, get ready to see Orlando's natural wonders.

Chapter 6

Arts And Culture

Orlando, the city famed for its captivating theme parks and active nightlife, also has a diversified and growing arts and entertainment sector that frequently goes unnoticed.

This chapter covers the cultural assets that make Orlando a destination for anyone seeking a more sophisticated and creative experience, from world-class museums to compelling performing arts venues.

Orlando Museum of Art (OMA)

...Nurturing Creativity in the Sun
@ 2416 N. Mills Ave., Orlando, FL 32803.
Among Orlando's sparkling attractions and captivating theme parks, the Orlando Museum of Art (OMA) shines as a radiant light of culture and innovation.

Since its inception in 1924, this venerable institution has served as a bedrock of artistic appreciation and education in Central Florida. You may escape the hustle and bustle of Orlando's tourist attractions and immerse yourself in the world of art here.

A Sneak Peek at the OMA's Artistic Tapestry

The Orlando Museum of Art houses an exquisitely curated collection spanning continents and centuries. This magnificent collection exemplifies the vast range of artistic expression and thinking. Here are some highlights from the OMA experience:

The American Art

Stepping inside the American art department of the OMA is like embarking on a voyage through the annals of American history and culture.

Admire the timeless works of renowned American artists like Georgia O'Keeffe, whose bright landscapes reflect the spirit of the American Southwest, and John Singer Sargent, a portraiture master whose brushstrokes caught the soul of the Gilded Age.

African Art

The OMA's African art collection draws visitors into a world of mystery and meaning. It is an enthralling overview of the continent's different cultures.

From beautifully carved masks that disclose ancestral connections to vivid textiles that communicate community stories, this collection exemplifies African artistry's beauty and resourcefulness.

Contemporary Art

OMA does not just look back; it actively embraces the present and future of artistic expression. The museum organizes vibrant exhibitions of contemporary art on a regular basis, giving new artists a forum to share their views and ideas.

These shows add new views and thought provoking notions to the OMA experience. Beyond its amazing collection, the OMA serves as an important educational hub. It provides a variety of interesting programs and courses aimed at inspiring creativity in both children and adults.

The museum is dedicated to cultivating the artistic spirit in the Orlando community, offering anything from art workshops to interactive meetings with artists.

Ticket Costs

Adults pay $15.
Seniors (65 and up): $8
Students (with valid ID): $5
Children (4-17 years old): $5
Members and children under the age of four: Free

The Orlando Museum of Art is more than just a gallery; it is a haven for creativity and a testament to the enduring power of human expression.

You will be transported through time and space as you tour its galleries, gaining fresh insights into the world of art.

So, whether you are a seasoned art aficionado or simply looking for a break from Orlando's vivid pandemonium, OMA invites you to bask in the warmth of creative beauty and inspiration amidst the Florida sunlight.

Dr. Phillips Center For Performing Arts

@ 445 S. Magnolia Ave., Orlando, FL 32801.
The Dr. Phillips Center for the Performing Arts, located in the center of downtown Orlando, is both an architectural masterpiece and a cultural gem.

This performing arts facility, which opened in 2014, exemplifies Orlando's dedication to promoting and honoring artistic achievement.

It has since become an iconic emblem of the city's booming cultural scene, with a broad selection of performances catering to a wide range of tastes and interests.

Architectural magnificence

The remarkable architecture of the Dr. Phillips Center is a work of art in and of itself. With its sleek glass façade and angular, curvilinear curves, the facility was designed by world-renowned architect Barton Myers to have a modern, yet timeless appeal.

The structure blends perfectly with Orlando's skyline, creating a welcoming ambiance that invites visitors to explore its aesthetic treasures.

The Locations

There are two principal performance halls within the Dr. Phillips Center, both precisely built to improve the audience's experience:

The Walt Disney Theater is the center's crown gem, with a seating capacity of nearly 2,700 people. Its design emphasizes acoustic precision, ensuring that every note of a symphony orchestra or every line of a Broadway production may be heard clearly.

Legendary performers, world-class orchestras, and some of Broadway's most acclaimed plays have all graced the stage.

The Alexis & Jim Pugh Theater has seating for up to 300 people and is ideal for a more intimate encounter.

This smaller facility is perfect for chamber music, dance recitals, and smaller-scale theater shows. Its design allows for a deeper interaction between performers and audience members, resulting in an immersive and engaging environment.

The Plaza Outside

The Dr. Phillips Center has an appealing outdoor plaza in addition to its indoor splendors. This lively location frequently holds free community events, live music performances, and meetings.

It is a bustling hub of activity, ideal for pre-show gatherings, post-performance chats, or simply unwinding in the heart of downtown Orlando.

Ticket Costs

Ticket costs at the Dr. Phillips Center vary greatly based on the event's nature and popularity.

Premium tickets for top-tier Broadway performances and globally famous concerts can cost from $200 to $500 or more, while smaller theater productions may start at around $25.

The center also offers subscription packages and student discounts, making it accessible to a wide range of clients.

The Dr. Phillips Center for the Performing Arts is a cultural and creative hotspot in Orlando. Its dedication to excellence in architectural design and creative programming has solidified it as a world-class destination for performing arts fans.

Charles Hosmer Morse Museum of American Art

Located at Winter Park, FL 32789 (445 N. Park Ave.), the Charles Hosmer Morse Museum of American Art is a hidden treasure of artistic splendor.

The Charles Hosmer Morse Museum of American Art stands as a tribute to the enduring fascination of artistic greatness, nestled among the charming and lovely streets of Winter Park, just a short drive from downtown Orlando.

This cultural treasure has constantly delighted tourists with its amazing dedication to maintaining the artistic legacy of one of the world's most recognized decorative arts figures: Louis Comfort Tiffany.

Louis Comfort Tiffany Tribute

The Morse Museum is an exceptional testament to Louis Comfort Tiffany's unparalleled talent, a name synonymous with stunning stained glass works and creative decorative art.

As you enter the museum's hallowed corridors, you are taken to a realm where light, color, and design blend to create ethereal beauty.

The Tiffany Collection

The Morse Museum houses the world's most extensive collection of Tiffany's works. This includes his famed stained glass windows, brilliant lamps, finely created jewelry, and a plethora of ornamental goods that continue to astonish and amaze.

The beautiful chapel interior, originally designed for the 1893 World's Columbian Exposition in Chicago, is one of the museum's crown jewels. Its very presence is enough to captivate visitors, as it exudes spiritual serenity via the magnificent dance of light and color.

Extravaganza of American Art Nouveau

While the Morse Museum's Tiffany collection is certainly its greatest splendor, there is much more to discover beyond the works of this remarkable artist.

The museum houses an extraordinary collection of American Art Nouveau artifacts that capture the essence of a late nineteenth and early twentieth century art and design movement.

These items, which range from delicate jewelry to ornate ornamental artifacts, provide visitors with an insight of the era's luxury and ingenuity.

Diverse Decorative Arts

The Morse Museum is not just about Tiffany and Art Nouveau. You will find a wide range of ornamental arts in its treasure trove, including pottery, ceramics, and furniture.

These meticulously picked and presented pieces highlight the craftsmanship and design sensibility that marked several periods in American art history.

Time and Art on a Journey

As you walk through the galleries of the Morse Museum, you will be taken on a mesmerizing journey through time and artistry.

Each piece on display tells a story, whether it is a Tiffany masterpiece or a tribute to the larger artistic movements that created America's cultural landscape.

Ticket Costs

Adults pay $6.
Seniors (60 and up): $5
Students (with valid ID): $1
Children under the age of 12 are free.

The Charles Hosmer Morse Museum of American Art is a haven of beauty, craftsmanship, and historical relevance. It enables you to become immersed in Tiffany's fascinating world as well as the larger tapestry of American decorative arts.

A voyage through a realm where artistry transcends time and the history of creative greatness continues to amaze and inspire.

Whether you are an art enthusiast, a history buff, or simply looking for aesthetic pleasure, the Morse Museum in Winter Park promises a unique experience.

Harry P. Leu Gardens

...A Botanical Paradise

Orlando is well-known for its exhilarating theme parks and entertainment, but it also boasts a hidden gem that provides a calm getaway from the city's hustle and bustle.

The Harry P. Leu Gardens, nestled within the metropolitan landscape, is a floral paradise that invites visitors to immerse themselves in the calm of nature's splendor. We shall go deep into the magical world of this garden, named after its visionary founder, *Harry P. Leu*, in this section.

A Horticultural Paradise

The Harry P. Leu Gardens, which spans an amazing 50 acres, is a tribute to the city's commitment to preserving and presenting the natural world's magnificence. Stepping onto the professionally designed grounds transports you to a world of vivid hues, aromatic blossoms, and mesmerizing foliage.

Highlights

The Rose Garden reigns supreme among the grounds' numerous attractions. Its nearly 200 rose varietals are a monument to the craftsmanship and dedication of the garden's custodians. Visitors can wander along exquisite pathways, surrounded by the lovely aroma of fully bloomed roses.

The Tropical Stream Garden is a captivating delight for visitors seeking a taste of the tropics. Meandering streams are flanked with exotic vegetation that thrive in Florida's tropical climate. It is a sliver of paradise, delivering a glimpse of the Sunshine State's verdant beauty.

The Camellia Collection is a magnificent extravaganza not to be missed during the winter months. When other plants are dormant, these magnificent, evergreen shrubs explode into vivid colors, making for a remarkable and unforgettable visit.

The Tourist Experience

Visitors can enter this horticultural paradise by purchasing tickets at the gate. The following is the pricing structure:

Ticket Costs
Adults pay $10.
Seniors (65 and older): $5
Children (4-17 years old): $3
Children under the age of four are free.

Guided tours are offered for an additional cost for those interested in learning more about the garden's history and the vast array of plant life it houses. These excursions are given by knowledgeable professionals who add perspective to the garden's splendors.

Advice for Visitors

Consider the following suggestions to make the most of your visit to the Harry P. Leu Gardens:

- Wear comfortable walking shoes since you will want to explore every nook and cranny of this sprawling landscape.
- Sunscreen and hydration are critical, especially during the summer.
- Keep a watch on the garden's website for seasonal events and plant sales, which can provide extra opportunities to interact with the garden's products.

The Harry P. Leu Gardens, located in the center of Orlando, is a tribute to the city's commitment to conserving nature's beauty.

This horticultural sanctuary allows you to delight in the wonders of the natural world, whether you are a botany enthusiast, a nature lover, or simply looking for a calm refuge from the excitement of Orlando's theme parks.

Take your time, enjoy the scenery, and make memories among the bright flora of the Harry P. Leu Gardens.

Mennello Museum of American Art

Overview of the Mennello Museum of American Art: Where the American Art Comes to Life.

The Mennello Museum of American Art, located in the middle of gorgeous Loch Haven Park, is a testimony to the strength and beauty of American ingenuity.

Since its inception in 1998, this museum has become a destination for art fans, historians, and families looking for a one-of-a-kind cultural experience.

The Diverse Collections

The Mennello Museum houses an extraordinary collection spanning decades and styles, celebrating the many dimensions of American art.

Its permanent collection includes over 300 paintings, sculptures, and decorative arts, with a special emphasis on the works of self-taught American folk artist Earl Cunningham.

Cunningham's vivid, whimsical works offer an intriguing peek into the artistic mood of the American South.

Exhibits To Pique Your Interest

Aside from its outstanding permanent collection, the museum organizes a diverse range of special exhibitions. These exhibitions feature a diverse range of American art, from traditional to contemporary.

Visitors can expect to see works that highlight societal themes, reflect contemporary trends, and push artistic boundaries. It demonstrates the museum's dedication to displaying the shifting landscape of American inventiveness.

The Sculpture Garden of Marilyn L. Mennello

The Marilyn L. Mennello Sculpture Garden is one of the museum's most attractive features. This tranquil outdoor location complements the indoor exhibitions by allowing visitors to connect with art in nature.

Stroll through beautiful gardens that are embellished with intriguing sculptures, resulting in a harmonic blend of flora and artistic expression.

Visitor Interaction

Visitors of all ages and ethnicities are welcome at the Mennello Museum of American Art. Its approachable and intimate atmosphere makes it a great location for both art lovers and families looking for a culturally enriching experience.

Admission rates are modest, making it a viable alternative for both budget-conscious travelers and locals.

Ticket Costs

Adults pay $10.
Seniors (65 and older): $5
Free for active military personnel (with ID).
Children (6-17 years old): $1
On the second Sunday of each month, children under the age of six are admitted free, as are all visitors.

To enhance the tourist experience, the museum offers docent-led tours that provide insightful information about the artwork and the artists who created it.

Visiting Tips

- Before you go, check the museum's website for information on current exhibitions as well as any special events or programs.

- Consider visiting during the monthly ***"Free Family Funday"*** to enjoy the museum's offerings without paying admission.

The museum is conveniently positioned within Loch Haven Park, which also houses other cultural organizations and scenic lake views. Spend some additional time exploring the park's environs and the attractive neighborhood surrounding it.

When you enter the Mennello Museum of American Art, you will start on an enthralling journey through the diverse fabric of American craftsmanship.

 You can get drawn to Earl Cunningham's folk art, the constantly changing special exhibitions, or the serenity of the sculpture garden. This cultural treasure provides a window into the soul of American inventiveness that should not be missed during your vacation to Orlando.

Shakespeare Theater

Bringing Shakespeare' Legacy to Life
The Orlando Shakespeare Theater, is nestled within the beautiful embrace of Loch Haven Park, and

stands as a beacon of culture and the performing arts in the center of Orlando.

This tiny theater, frequently lauded as one of the city's cultural gems, provides an appealing getaway from the rush of theme parks, allowing guests to immerse themselves in the timeless worlds of Shakespeare and contemporary drama.

We go deeper into the enthralling world of the Orlando Shakespeare Theater in this segment.

A Classical and Contemporary Dramatic World

The Classic Shakespearean Plays

The Orlando Shakespeare Theater takes its name seriously, with a repertory that delves into William Shakespeare's masterpieces.

You will be taken to Elizabethan England or the mythological regions of Verona and Illyria as the lights dim and the curtain rises. ***"Romeo and Juliet," "Hamlet," and "Macbeth"*** are just a handful of Shakespeare's classics that have graced the stage here.

The Shakespearean prose is as brilliant as ever, and the ageless themes of love, power, and tragedy are brought to life in a manner that only live theater can.

Beyond the classics, the theater embraces modern theatre, bringing audiences to thought provoking and imaginative performances.

Each production promises a new viewpoint on the human experience, whether it is a modern reinterpretation of a Shakespearean play or a daring new work by a contemporary playwright.

The juxtaposition of classic and contemporary shows provides depth and variety to the theater's offerings, appealing to a diverse audience.

A Learning Center for Aspiring Thespians

The Orlando Shakespeare Theater is more than simply a place to watch plays; it is also a training ground for aspiring actors and theater fans.

The mission of the theater is centered on educational programs, workshops, and outreach efforts. Here's what to expect:

Educational Programs: The theater offers educational programs for students of all ages, from school groups to those who want to learn more about the dramatic arts.

These programs seek to deconstruct Shakespeare and theater in general, making the Bard's works accessible and interesting to all.

Community Involvement: The theater regularly connects with the local community by arranging outreach events and workshops that build an appreciation for theater and the performing arts.

The Orlando Shakespeare Theater plays an important role in defining the cultural landscape of the region by cultivating the talents of the next generation of actors, directors, and playwrights.

A Unique Theatrical Experience
When you enter the Orlando Shakespeare Theater, you are not only attending a performance; you are also becoming a part of a centuries-old tradition. Here are a few highlights of the theater experience:

Ticket Prices: Ticket costs for Orlando Shakespeare Theater events vary depending on the play and seating. Regular adult tickets normally vary from $25 and $60, with several alternatives to fit your preferences and budget. Students, elderly, and military people are eligible for discounts.

The Orlando Shakespeare Theater is distinguished by its intimate environment. The comfortable auditorium ensures that every seat in the house has a great view of the stage.

This proximity to the actors offers an immersive experience, allowing you to feel the performance's emotions, energy, and nuances up close and personal.

Advance Ticket Purchases

Due to the theater's popularity and limited capacity, it is best to purchase your tickets in advance, especially for highly anticipated plays. This guarantees you a seat to enjoy the wonder of live theater in this charming setting.

The Orlando Shakespeare Theater promises to take you to worlds both classic and contemporary. Prepare to be captivated by the spoken word's power, the craft of storytelling, and the eternal attraction of the theater.

Chapter 7

Dining and Culinary Delights

The Culinary Scene in Orlando

The "Theme Park Capital of the World" is not only a shelter for thrill seekers, but also a gourmet heaven for foodies.

The complex tapestry of cultures and influences that have molded the city's thriving community is reflected in its diversified culinary scene. Whether you choose exotic food or local favorites, Orlando has something for everyone.

International Cuisines

...from Around the World
Orlando is a varied and eclectic city, and its food scene reflects this. Whether you like Thai, Italian, Japanese, or Mexican food, there are plenty of international eating alternatives to suit your taste buds.

Here are some famous international restaurants and dining experiences in Orlando to try:

SEA Thai Restaurant's Cuisine

SEA Thai Restaurant takes you on a delicious tour through the flavors of Thailand. Their menu features a wide variety of traditional Thai cuisine, ranging from scrumptious

Pad Thai to fragrant green and red curries. The environment is welcoming and pleasant, making it ideal for a romantic supper or a family gathering.

A supper for two, including appetizers and main meals, normally costs between $40 and $60.

Prato's Italian Excellence Cuisine

Prato is a trendy Italian restaurant in the center of Winter Park, just north of Orlando. They are well-known for their wood-fired pizzas, homemade pasta, and ingredients obtained locally. The rustic yet modern design of the restaurant creates a pleasant ambiance that matches the great food.

Expect to pay between $50 and $80 for a supper for two, including a bottle of wine.

Sushi Sensations At Kabooki Sushi

Kabooki Sushi is a must-visit for sushi fans. This contemporary Japanese restaurant puts a unique spin on traditional sushi rolls and sashimi. The presentation is as good as the food, making it a popular choice for date evenings and special occasions.

A sushi meal for two, with appetizers and beverages, can cost between $60 and $100.

Black Rooster Taqueria's Authentic Mexican Flavors

Black Rooster Taqueria brings the bright flavors of Mexico to Orlando. Their cuisine includes street tacos, tamales, and delectable guacamole. The relaxed and colorful atmosphere enhances the overall experience, making it a local favorite.

Price Range: A tasty Mexican supper for two will cost you between $30 and $50, depending on your options.

Local Favorites

While Orlando is recognized for its international food, it also features a diverse range of local favorites that reflect Florida's distinct culture and flavors. Here are a few must-try local cuisine and restaurants:

The Rusty Spoon

Celebrates Florida's Iconic Citrus

Florida is famed for its citrus fruits, and The Rusty Spoon honors this tradition. For a taste of regional food, try their Florida Citrus Salad, which has locally produced oranges and grapefruits, or their Gator Bites.

Price range: Starters and small plates start around $10, while main meals run from $20 to $40.

Cuban Delights at Black Bean Deli

Visit Black Bean Deli for a taste of Cuba. They provide delicious Cuban sandwiches, empanadas, and rice bowls. It is a laid-back location ideal for a quick and excellent lunch.

Price: A hefty Cuban sandwich and a side dish will set you back less than $10.

The Boathouse Florida Seafood Extravaganza

The Boathouse, located at Disney Springs, offers a traditional Florida seafood experience. You can dine on fresh seafood such as oysters, crab legs, and shrimp while facing the picturesque lake. They also provide Amphicar tours for a one-of-a-kind dining experience.

Seafood meals range in price from $30 to $60, with appetizers and drinks adding to the total.

The Coop's Southern Comfort Food

The Coop specializes in Southern comfort food. Enjoy fried chicken, biscuits and gravy, collard greens, and other Southern comfort foods. The warm and inviting ambiance adds to the appeal.

A full Southern supper for two will normally cost between $30 and $50.

Food Trucks and Street Eats

...Food Truck Fever

Orlando's food truck culture has taken the city by storm, delivering a diverse range of flavors and cuisines in a casual, often low-cost setting. Here are some of Orlando's must-see food trucks and street eats:

The Daily Poutine Cuisine

Canadian-inspired poutine Price: $10 - $15 per *Location*: Disney Springs

Enjoy this Canadian classic with a Florida spin. The Daily Poutine offers fresh, crispy french fries topped with tasty gravy and cheese curds. It is the ideal comfort food to fuel your Disney adventure.

Tako Cheena

At Mills 50 is where you will find us. Tacos and sandwiches with Asian-Latin fusion are available at District Cuisine.

Tako Cheena is a local favorite recognized for its innovative and reasonably priced fusion cuisine.

For a unique and delectable experience, try their Korean BBQ tacos or tofu banh mi.

Price ranges from $3-$8 per piece

The Milk District Food Truck Bazaar
Location: The Milk District (Varies)
Cuisine: Various, with numerous food trucks
Price varies according to vendor.

If you are searching for diversity, go to The Milk District Food Truck Bazaar, where a rotating lineup of food trucks serves anything from gourmet grilled cheese to real Colombian arepas.

Flavors from Around the World

Orlando's food truck scene is highly diversified, with foreign cuisines from all over the world available. You may sample various flavors without leaving the city, from Cuban sandwiches to Korean BBQ.

Most food truck products cost between $5 and $15, making them a good choice for frugal visitors.

Fine Dining and Upscale Restaurants

Orlando has a booming fine dining industry in addition to its casual eateries. You can discover a variety of luxury restaurants to select from, whether you are celebrating a special event or simply looking for a great culinary experience.

Victoria & Albert's.

Location: Disney's Grand Floridian Resort & Spa
Cuisine: American, Contemporary, & International
Price Per Person: $235 - $250 (multiple-course prix fixe)

Book a reservation at Victoria & Albert's, a AAA Five Diamond Award-winning restaurant, for a genuinely opulent dining experience.

The prix fixe menu includes expertly made meals, and the sophisticated ambiance is ideal for a romantic evening.

Napa

Location: Four Seasons Resort.
Cuisines: Californian and Mediterranean
Prices range from $50 to $80 per person (à la carte).

The Four Seasons Resort in Napa Valley has a stunning view of the golf course. This restaurant is great for individuals who like modern American cuisine, with a menu that emphasizes fresh, seasonal ingredients.

The Waldorf Astoria

Bull & Bear Steakhouse
Steakhouse Cuisine in Orlando
Prices range from $50 to $150 per person (à la carte).

Bull & Bear Steakhouse is a great option for meat enthusiasts. This upmarket restaurant, known for its excellent steaks and large wine list, guarantees a great dining experience.

Vegetarian and Vegan Options

Café Dandelion Communitea

Dandelion Communitea Café, located in the center of Orlando's Thornton Park, is a pleasant, eco-friendly eatery noted for its organic, vegetarian, and vegan meals.

For roughly $12, try their "Bodhi Bowl" with mixed greens, quinoa, and a variety of veggies topped with homemade tahini dressing.

Vegan Kitchen Ethos

This well-known vegan restaurant serves a broad cuisine that includes vegan mac 'n' cheese, BBQ jackfruit sandwiches, and sumptuous desserts. A hearty lunch at the Vegan Kitchen Ethos should cost between $10 and $15.

Market On The South

Market on South is a one-of-a-kind experience that combines a vegan restaurant, a bakery, and a local goods market. Try their "Vegan Fried Chicken" sandwich for approximately $12, followed by a tasty vegan donut for about $3.

Tea Infusion

This quaint tea business not only serves a broad assortment of teas, but also vegetarian and vegan options. For about $10, you can get a filling veggie wrap or a vegan chili bowl.

Market On Plant Street

Plant Street Market, located in neighboring Winter Garden, is a food hall with various kiosks offering vegetarian and vegan options. Plant-based sushi to vegan tacos are available, with prices ranging from $10 to $15 per item.

Craft Beer and Breweries

The craft beer sector in Orlando is developing, with a rising number of breweries and taprooms offering a diverse assortment of brews. Here are some of the best places in town to enjoy craft beer:

Crooked Can Brewing Corporation

This Winter Garden brewery is well-known for its European-style beers and a lovely outside sitting area. A pint of artisan beer here will cost you between $6 and $8.

Orlando Brewing Company

As Orlando's oldest brewery, this is a must-see for beer enthusiasts. A brewery tour costs about $10, and you can sample their organic, handcrafted brews starting at $5 per pint.

Dead Lizard Brewing Company

Dead Lizard, a local favorite, offers a diverse assortment of unique beer varieties. A flight of beers costs roughly $10, and a pint costs $5-$7.

Larder & Cask

Cask & Larder is a brewery and Southern-inspired restaurant located in Orlando International Airport. Expect to pay between $7 and $9 for their artisan beers, which combine wonderfully with their delectable culinary options.

The Hourglass Brewing Company

Hourglass Brewing, known for its innovative and experimental brews, has a rotating tap roster. A pint usually costs between $6 and $8.

Wineries and Distilleries

Lakeridge Winery & Vineyards

19239 US Highway 27 North, Clermont, FL 34715
Lakeridge Winery & Vineyards is one of Florida's largest and most famous vineyards, nestled among the rolling hills of Clermont, just a short drive from downtown Orlando.

It is well-known for producing a wide range of wines, particularly those made from the region's unique Muscadine grapes. Visitors can take advantage of free tours and tastings to learn about the winemaking process and try their award-winning wines.

Cost for Complimentary tours and tastings; wine costs range from roughly $10 per bottle.

Quantum Leap Winery

1312 Wilfred Drive, Orlando, FL 32803.
Quantum Leap Winery is not just a destination for wine connoisseurs, but it is also an eco-friendly company with a mission to encourage sustainable winemaking processes.

They acquire fruit from vineyards all around the world, resulting in a vast range of wines with distinct characteristics. The tasting area provides a pleasant environment in which to sample their wines and learn about their environmentally friendly approach.

Price Estimates: Tasting flights start at $12 per person, and wine bottles range in price.

The Rogue Pig

Winter Park, FL 32789, 565 W. Fairbanks Avenue
While officially a gastropub, The Ravenous Pig has an excellent assortment of craft beers and drinks, as well as an extensive wine list that complements their imaginative cuisine.

This restaurant is a sanctuary for foodies and wine lovers alike, thanks to its premium yet approachable cooking. Throughout the year, they offer wine dinners and unique events.

Wine by the glass starts at $10; bottles range in price; food costs vary depending on menu items.

Winter Park Distilling Company.

Winter Park, FL 32789, 1288 N. Orange Avenue
If you are more of a spirits fan, stop by Winter Park Distilling Company for a taste of locally created spirits.

This micro-distillery specializes in small-batch, handcrafted spirits like vodka, gin, and bourbon. A distillery tour allows you to witness the production process up close and enjoy sampling.

Distillery tours and tastings start at $10 per person, and bottle prices vary.

Broken Cauldron Taproom & Brewery

1012 West Church Street, Orlando, FL 32805
The Broken Cauldron Taproom & Brewery is a must-see for anybody interested in artisan beer.

While it is not a vineyard or distillery, it is a local treasure recognized for its broad assortment of beers, which includes their own creations as well as guest brews. It is a fantastic spot to unwind after a day of seeing because of the pleasant ambiance and courteous personnel.

Price Estimates: Beer costs start at $6 per pint and go up from there; flights are available.

Chapter 8

Nightlife And Entertainment

Orlando is more than just theme parks and family-friendly activities; it comes alive after dark with a thriving nightlife and a diverse choice of entertainment alternatives.

Orlando provides something for everyone, whether you like live music, dancing, or supper and a show. Come along through the bustling nightlife scene and get ready to have the greatest nighttime experience.

Nightlife in Downtown Orlando

Wall Street Plaza

Located in the heart of downtown Orlando, Wall Street Plaza is a buzzing entertainment complex with a variety of pubs, restaurants, and clubs.

It is a popular hangout for both locals and tourists looking for a good time. There will be live music, DJ sets, and themed parties. Drink prices vary, but expect to pay $5-10 for a beer and $8-15 for a cocktail.

Church Street

Lined with taverns, clubs, and restaurants, this ancient street. Church Street is well-known for its establishments such as "The Beacham," a classic nightclub that hosts live music and special events.

Ticket and drink prices will vary based on the event, but a normal night out may cost between $15 and $25.

Elixir Orlando

If you want handmade cocktails in a more premium setting, Elixir Orlando is an excellent choice. The bartenders at this establishment are well-known for their inventive concoctions.
Cocktails often cost between $12 and $15.

The Social

The Social is a tiny and intimate venue for indie music fans that showcases live events by local and touring artists. Ticket prices vary but are often between $10 and $20. The prices of the drinks are reasonable.

Amway Center

If you happen to be in Orlando during a major performance or event at the Amway Center, it is an entertainment experience unlike any other.

Ticket prices vary widely depending on the act, so expect to pay between $50 and $200 for a ticket.

The International Drive Entertainment

@ ICON Park

ICON Park is an entertainment complex on International Drive that includes restaurants, shopping, and attractions.

The 400-foot-tall observation tower known as The tower provides stunning views of the city. The Wheel tickets normally cost $27-30 for adults and $22-25 for children.

The Pointe Orlando

Pointe Orlando, another renowned entertainment complex on International Drive, has a variety of restaurants, bars, and stores.

You can watch a movie at Regal Cinemas or listen to live music on the Main Stage. Prices for meals and entertainment vary, but they are often reasonable.

Mango's Tropical Cafe

Get a taste of the tropics with live music, dancing, and a Latin-inspired dinner show at Mango's Tropical Cafe. The cover charge is typically $25-30 per person, and dinner costs begin around $30-40 per entree.

Themed Dinner Shows

Medieval Times meal & Tournament

Immerse yourself in the medieval age with an exciting meal and entertainment featuring jousting, sword fights, and a feast fit for a king at Medieval Times.

Adult tickets cost roughly $60-70, while children's tickets cost around $36-47.

Pirate's Dinner voyage

Set sail on a swashbuckling voyage at Pirate's Dinner Adventure, where you will feast on a three-course meal while watching a pirate-themed show.

Adult tickets cost between $50 and $70, while children's tickets cost between $30 and $40.

Sleuths Mystery Dinner Shows

For those who enjoy a good mystery, Sleuths Mystery Dinner Shows provide participatory entertainment with a comic twist.

Adult tickets start at $62 and children's tickets start around $29, including dinner.

Live Music Venues

Orlando has a thriving live music scene that features a diverse spectrum of musical styles. You will find a place to fit your tastes, whether you like rock, jazz, blues, hip-hop, or electronic dance music. Here are some of Orlando's best live music venues:

House Of Blues

The House of Blues, located in Disney Springs, is a legendary venue that features both national and local performances. The cozy setting and great sound system make it a favorite among music fans.

Ticket costs vary by artist but often ranges from $20 to $100 or more.

The Social

This downtown Orlando venue is well-known for its indie and alternative music. It is a smaller, more intimate environment ideal for discovering new talent.

Typical ticket costs ranges from $10 to $30.

Hard Rock Live

Located at the Universal Orlando Resort, Hard Rock Live is a large facility that draws notable performances from a variety of genres.

Tickets for lesser performances might range from $30 to $100 or more for big-name acts.

The Beacham

The Beacham is a prominent nightclub and live music venue located on historic Orange Avenue in downtown Orlando. It frequently holds DJ parties as well as live performances.
Ticket costs ranges from $15 to $50 on average.

Dr. Phillips Center for the Performing Arts

If you want a more upscale music experience, go to the Dr. Phillips Center. This cutting-edge facility hosts classical performances, Broadway plays, and well-known singers.
Ticket costs ranges from $30 to $200 or more depending on the event and seats.

Comedy Clubs

...Laughter Lounges

Orlando's comedy culture is growing, with multiple venues hosting stand-up events and improv acts that are sure to make you laugh. Here are some of the best comedy clubs in town:

Sak Comedy Lab

Sak Comedy Lab, located in downtown Orlando, is known for its amazing improv comedy presentations. Tickets are typically priced between

$10 and $20. It is a great option for a night of laughs with friends.

Improv Orlando

Located on International Drive, Improv Orlando attracts both established and emerging comedians from all over the country. Ticket costs vary with the act but typically range from $15 to $40.

Bonkerz comedic Club

Bonkerz has several locations in Orlando and offers a variety of comedic experiences. Various locations in the city host stand-up performers, with ticket prices ranging from $10 to $25.

The Other Bar Comedy Club

Located in downtown Orlando, this intimate comedy club presents stand-up comedy shows and open mic evenings. Tickets are reasonably priced, typically ranging from $5 to $15.

SAK Comedy Lab

Known for its funny improv comedy acts, the SAK Comedy Lab in downtown Orlando provides a fun night out. Tickets are typically priced between $10 and $20.

Nightclubs and Bars

Clubs and Taverns

EVE Orlando

Located at 110 S Orange Ave, Orlando, FL 32801.
EVE Orlando is an upscale nightclub located in the center of downtown Orlando. It is popular among the city's partygoers thanks to its upmarket décor, world-class DJs, and big dance floor. Expect a trendy audience with a mix of electronic dance music and top 40 tunes.

Cover rates vary but are normally between $20 and $30. Drinks cost between $10 and $15.

The Courtesy Bar

Address is 114 N Orange Ave, Orlando, FL 32801.
The Courtesy Bar is the place to go if you are looking for creative cocktails in a cozy setting. Their professional mixologists use fresh ingredients to make distinctive and delicious beverages. The easygoing ambiance makes it ideal for a laid-back evening.
Cocktails start at about $12, and here there is no cover charge.

Tier Nightclub

20 E Central Blvd, Orlando, FL 32801
Description: Tier Nightclub is known for its cutting-edge sound system and eye-catching

lighting effects. EDM fans will have a great time partying the night away here. Check the club's schedule for special events since they frequently feature internationally renowned DJs.

Prices: Cover costs range from $10 to $30. Drinks begin at $10.

Park Avenue Wine Room

Address: 270 S Park Ave, Winter Park, FL 32789
Head to The Wine Room on Park Avenue for a more refined evening. This wine bar serves a wide variety of wines by the glass, making it ideal for wine lovers and those looking for a refined night out.

Wine by the glass prices vary, but expect to pay $8-15 per glass.

Wall Street Plaza

Location: 25 Wall St, Orlando, FL 32801
Wall Street Plaza is a busy entertainment complex that houses a variety of pubs and eateries. You can go from venue to venue while listening to live music, dancing, and meeting new people. It is a good choice for **bar hoppers**.

Cover Charges: Some establishments may impose a cover charge. The pricing of drinks vary, although they are often reasonable.

Family-Friendly Evening Activities

Disney Springs

1486 Buena Vista Dr, Orlando, FL 32830

Disney Springs is a family-friendly entertainment district that provides a fantastic setting with shopping, dining, and entertainment opportunities. Discover unusual shops, take in the streets' entertainment, and sample delectable delicacies.

Admission to Disney Springs is free, however prices for food and shopping vary.

The Orlando Science Center After Dark

Location: 777 E Princeton St, Orlando, FL 32803

If your family enjoys science and learning, you should consider attending the Orlando Science Center After Dark event. It is an interactive, educational experience with live science presentations and interactive exhibits.

Ticket prices range from $20 to $25 for adults and $15 to $20 for children.

Pirate's Cove Adventure Golf

Location: Various sites, including 8501 International Dr, Orlando, FL 32819

Mini golf is a great family-friendly evening activity, and Pirate's Cove Adventure Golf offers themed courses with pirate adventures. It is a fun and challenging way to spend time with your friends.

Prices vary each region but are normally between $12 and $15 per person.

Cirque Magique Dinner Show

6400 Carrier Dr, Orlando, FL 32819
The Cirque Magique Dinner Show blends magic, comedy, and circus performances to provide an engaging and family-friendly evening out. Enjoy a wonderful meal while watching the performances.

Ticket prices range from $30 and $35 for adults and $20 to $25 for children.

Chapter 9

Shopping And Getting Around

Shoppin' Orlando

When it comes to shopping, Orlando has a wide variety of intriguing options for travelers to enjoy. This city provides something for any shopper's taste and budget, from world-class shopping areas to outlet malls and unique souvenir shops.

Shopping Districts

Luxury Shopping At Millenia Mall

The Mall at Millenia is Orlando's leading luxury shopping destination, located just minutes from Universal Orlando Resort and Walt Disney World.

This upmarket mall has an excellent array of high-end brands including Gucci, Louis Vuitton, and Chanel, making it a luxury shopping heaven. Even if you do not want to spend money, the mall is a terrific spot to go window shopping and people-watch.

Luxury shopping may be pricey, with things ranging from $100 to several thousand dollars.

However, there are some mid-priced stores and opportunities for more cheap shopping.

Disneyland Park

Disney Springs, formerly known as Downtown Disney, is an entertainment and shopping area at Walt Disney World Resort. It provides a one-of-a-kind mix of themed stores, boutiques, and dining experiences.

Everything Disney-related may be found here, from clothing to toys to collectibles and art. Stroll along the shoreline, listen to live music, and do not forget to stop by the massive World of Disney store for the ultimate Disney shopping experience.

Prices: The prices of Disney items vary greatly. T-shirts and souvenirs can cost as little as $15, while high-end memorabilia can cost hundreds of dollars.

I-Drive International Journey

International Drive, sometimes known as I-Drive, is a bustling tourist corridor with a wealth of shopping opportunities. Several shopping centers, including Pointe Orlando and ICON Park, can be found along this stretch.

These neighborhoods have a variety of retail stores, entertainment venues, and food alternatives. It is a great spot to buy souvenirs, apparel, and one-of-a-kind gifts.

Price Range: Prices vary substantially along I-Drive. There are inexpensive souvenirs and clothing, but there are also fancy shops and restaurants for people who want to indulge.

Orlando International Premium Outlets for Bargain Shopping

If you are looking for a good deal, Orlando International Premium Outlets is a must-see. This outlet mall has approximately 180 retailers, including well-known brands such as Nike, Coach, and Michael Kors, all of which offer up to 65% off regular retail pricing. Prepare for a day of treasure seeking and incredible bargains.

Prices: Discounts can be enormous, with most things much less expensive than at typical retail locations. Clothing, shoes, and accessories are frequently priced between $20 and $100.

Factory Stores in Lake Buena Vista

Lake Buena Vista Factory Stores is a great place to go for more affordable shopping. This outlet mall, located near Disney World, sells factory-direct clothing from well-known brands such as Gap, Levi's, and Calvin Klein. Prices are really low here, making it a fantastic spot to stock up on necessities or discover that perfect keepsake.

Approximate Prices: Clothing goods can be found for as little as $10, with reductions ranging from 30% to 70% off the original retail price.

Souvenirs And Gifts

For Souvenirs and gifts that are one-of-a-kind

Spice And Tea Exchange

The Spice & Tea Exchange in Winter Park offers a one-of-a-kind and aromatic shopping experience. This lovely business sells hand-mixed spices, herbs, gourmet teas, and one-of-a-kind seasoning combinations.

Beautiful kitchen accessories are also available, making it a great spot to pick either a memorable gift or something special for your own kitchen.

Spices and teas are moderately priced, with most items costing between $5 and $15.

The Market at East End

East End Market in Orlando's Audubon Park Garden District is a mecca for artisanal goods and handcrafted items. Explore a collection of tiny, independent stores that sell everything from handmade jewelry and candles to locally produced gourmet cuisine. It is a great place to find one of a kind gifts while also supporting local craftspeople.

Prices vary based on the vendor and product, but you can discover unusual gifts and goods for as little as $10.

Orlando genuinely caters to all types of shoppers, with its numerous shopping selections ranging from premium brands to outlet bargains and unique local treasures. So, when visiting this dynamic city, make time for some retail therapy. Have fun shopping!

Getting Around Orlando

Orlando, Florida is a large metropolis noted for its world-class attractions, entertainment, and scenic beauty. To make the most of your vacation, you must be able to navigate this dynamic city.

In this section, will look at several modes of transportation, such as hiring a car, taking public transportation, biking, walking, safety guidelines for tourists, and accessibility considerations.

Transportation Alternatives

Orlando has a variety of transportation alternatives to meet the demands of every visitor. There is something for everyone, whether you prefer the ease of hiring a car or wish to discover the city by eco friendly means like biking and walking.

Renting A Vehicle

Renting a car in Orlando is a popular option for many travelers because it allows you to explore the city and its attractions at your own pace. Consider the following important details:

Rental Car Companies: Hertz, Enterprise, Avis, and Budget have a strong presence in Orlando, with many locations at the airport and around the city.

To rent a car, you must have a valid driver's license, a credit card, and be at least 21 years old. Drivers under the age of 25 may face age restrictions and additional fees at some agencies.

Cost: Rental fees vary according to car model, duration, and insurance coverage. A basic car will cost you between $30 and $100 each day on average. Luxury and specialty automobiles will be more expensive.

Gas rates in Orlando are relatively low, with prices varying but generally average around $3.00 to $3.50 per gallon.

Parking: There are numerous parking alternatives in Orlando, including hotel parking, public garages, and street parking. property parking costs between $15 and $30 per day, depending on the property.

Public Transportation

If you prefer to use public transportation, there are various options in Orlando to help you travel around the city quickly such as:

LYNX Buses

The LYNX bus system serves a large portion of Orlando and adjacent areas. A one-way fee is roughly $2.00, while a day pass is approximately $4.50 and provides unlimited trips for the day.

SunRail

This commuter train service runs from DeBary to Poinciana and links numerous areas in Orlando. A one-way SunRail ticket costs between $2.00 and $7.00, depending on the distance traveled.

The I-Ride Trolley

This trolley service runs along International Drive and is helpful for guests exploring the tourism district. A single trip costs $2.00, while a day pass costs $5.00.

LYMMO

The LYMMO is a free downtown circulator bus system that serves Orlando's central business district, making it simple to explore the downtown region.

Cycling and walking

Biking and walking are wonderful options in Orlando for the ecologically concerned traveler or those who prefer a slower pace.

Biking

There is a growing network of bike lanes and trails in Orlando. You can ride throughout the city on bikes rented from several *bike-sharing programs such as Juice Bike Share*. Typical rental rates range from $5.00 to $8.00 per hour, or $15.00 to $25.00 per day.

Walking

Getting around Orlando on foot is a terrific way to see the city's colorful neighborhoods and stunning surroundings. Many neighborhoods, including downtown Orlando and Winter Park, are pedestrian friendly, with plenty of sidewalks and crosswalks.

Tourist Safety Recommendations

Orlando is a fairly secure city for tourists, however like with any other place, care must be taken to safeguard yourself and your items and belongings:

Keep an eye on your surrounds: Whether you are walking, riding, or taking public transportation, keep an eye on your surroundings, especially in congested places.

Keep your belongings secure: Always keep your belongings, such as wallets, purses, and cameras, secure. To deter pickpockets, wear a money belt or carry a safe bag.

Avoid poorly lighted or empty locations at night: If you are out late, stay to well-lit streets and avoid poorly lit or uninhabited areas.

Know the following emergency phone numbers: 911 is the primary emergency number in Orlando (list of emergency Contacts are outlined in chapter 10). Know your local emergency numbers and have a strategy in place in case of an emergency.

Orlando Accessibility

Orlando is committed to making its attractions accessible to all tourists, including those with disabilities. Here are some things to think about:

Accessibility

The majority of Orlando's major attractions, hotels, and public transportation are wheelchair accessible, with ramps, elevators, and accessible facilities.

Service Animals: Most Orlando attractions and businesses welcome service animals. Carry the essential documents for your service animal.

Accessible Transportation: Ramps and secure wheelchair spaces are available on Lynx buses and SunRail for passengers with mobility issues.

Many Orlando attractions, including theme parks such as Walt Disney World and Universal Orlando, provide accessible services such as wheelchair rentals and special access lines for disabled visitors.

Chapter 10

Practical Informations

Emergency Contacts

It is critical to know the emergency contact information before visiting Orlando in case of unexpected health difficulties. ***911 is the primary emergency number*** for medical assistance. Orlando's medical facilities are excellent, with various hospitals and clinics available. Here are some well-known healthcare facilities:

Orlando Health

Orlando Health is a significant healthcare provider that operates numerous hospitals throughout the city, including Orlando Regional Medical Center and Arnold Palmer Hospital for Children.

Contact: +1 321-841-5111
Address: 52 W. Underwood St., Orlando, FL 32806
Florida Hospital Orlando is a well-known hospital that offers a wide range of medical treatments.

601 East Rollins Street, Orlando, FL 32803
Phone: +1 407-303-5600
Law Enforcement and the Police

For non-medical emergencies or to report a crime, *dial 911 for quick assistance from the Orlando Police Department*. They are well-trained to manage a variety of circumstances and can provide advise if you have any safety concerns.

Vaccinations for Public Health and Safety

Check that your usual vaccines are up to date before flying to Orlando. It is also a good idea to consult with your doctor about any additional vaccines needed for travel to the region, especially if you are going during flu season.

Sun Protection

Orlando has a subtropical climate, which means it gets plenty of sun all year. Consider the following to shield yourself from the sun's harmful rays:

Sunscreen: Apply at least SPF 30 sunscreen on exposed skin, especially during outdoor activities.

Hydration: Stay hydrated by drinking plenty of water, especially during the hot summer months.

Sunglasses and hats: To protect your face and eyes from the sun, it is advisable to wear wide-brimmed hats and sunglasses.

Theft Prevention in Theme Parks

While the theme parks in Orlando are generally safe, it is important to take precautions, especially if you are visiting with children. Keep the following safety precautions in mind:

Children should be supervised at all times, especially in crowded places.

Stay Hydrated!

Dehydration can be an issue during long days in the parks, so drink plenty of water.

Observe the Park Rules: Follow all of the rules and instructions offered by the theme park staff.

Use Lockers: If you have valuables or items that you do not want to carry around with you, consider hiring lockers, which are accessible in most parks.

Etiquette and Tipping

Tipping is traditional in the United States, including Orlando. Here's a breakdown of who to tip and how much to tip:

Restaurants: The usual tip is 15% to 20% of the total cost. If the gratuity is not already included in the bill, it is customary to leave a tip.

Bartenders should be tipped 15% to 20% of the whole bill or $1 per drink, depending on the establishment.

Taxis and ride-hailing services: Tip 15% of the fare, rounded up to the nearest dollar.

Tour Guides: Depending on the length and quality of the tour, consider tipping the guide $5 to $10 per person.

Hotel Employees: It is usual to tip hotel employees who give great service. Tip housekeepers $2 to $5 per night and bellhops $2 to $5 per bag for carrying your bags.

Tip *Spa And Salon* personnel 15% to 20% of the total service fee.

Visitor Information Centers

Tourists can benefit greatly from the visitor centers in Orlando. They provide maps, brochures, and other useful information to make your stay more enjoyable. Among the notable visitor centers are:

- *Orlando Visitors Center*

8102 International Drive, Suite 100, Orlando, FL 32819
Services include maps, attraction tickets, and insider information.

- *Visitor Information at Orlando International Airport*

Orlando International Airport (MCO) Main Terminal Atrium

Services: Information about airport facilities and neighboring attractions is provided.

- *Visitor Information Desk at the Orange County Convention Center*

9800 International Dr., West Building, Level 1, Orlando, FL 32819

Services include event information and neighboring attractions.

These practical information will make it easier for you to traverse Orlando, assuring a safe and happy visit to this dynamic city.

Appendices

Sample Itineraries

One of the most exciting yet difficult aspects of arranging a vacation to Orlando is selecting how to make the most of your time in this diverse and exhilarating destination.

We have carefully crafted a variety of sample itineraries that appeal to varied interests and lengths of stay to help you navigate the plethora of attractions and activities Orlando has to offer.

These itineraries provide a solid foundation for a memorable journey, whether you are traveling with family, seeking thrills, or looking for a variety of activities.

(3 Days) Family Adventure

Day 1: Wonderful Beginnings

Morning: Begin your Orlando vacation with the splendor of Walt Disney World's Magic Kingdom. Adult tickets normally start around $109, while children aged 3 to 9 typically start around $103. The magnificent Cinderella Castle invites you to a magical world.

Lunch: Immerse yourself in a fantastic character eating experience at Cinderella's Royal Table, where prices vary from $65 to $95.

Afternoon: Wander through Fantasyland, Adventureland, and Tomorrowland. Classic rides like Space Mountain, where you will shoot off into space, and the swashbuckling Pirates of the Caribbean adventure are not to be missed.

Evening: Enjoy the amazing "Happily Ever After" fireworks and projection show, the ideal way to round off your first day in Orlando.

Day 2: Animal Encounters
Morning: Visit Disney's Animal Kingdom and immerse yourself in the delights of the animal kingdom.

Tickets for adults start about $109, and tickets for children aged 3 to 9 start around $103. Begin your day with a thrilling ride on the Expedition Everest roller coaster.

Lunch: In Asia, dine at the unique Yak & Yeti Restaurant, where prices normally vary from $15 to $35 per person.

Afternoon: Visit Pandora - The World of Avatar, which is home to the spectacular Avatar Flight of Passage rollercoaster. Do not miss out on the exciting Kilimanjaro Safaris and the hypnotic Rivers of Light nightly spectacle.

Evening: Cap off your day with the enchanting atmosphere of "Rivers of Light," a nocturnal spectacle that combines water, light, and music.

Day 3: Universal Studios Adventure

Morning: Visit the amazing world of Universal Orlando Resort, where adult tickets start at about $115 and children's tickets start at about $110. Begin your journey at Universal Studios Florida.

Lunch: Dine at The Leaky Cauldron in Diagon Alley, where prices normally range from $10 to $20 per person.

Afternoon: Explore The Wizarding World of Harry Potter, Transformers: The Ride 3D, and dare to venture through Jurassic Park.

Evening: Finish your wonderful Orlando vacation with "The Nighttime Lights at Hogwarts Castle," a stunning light and sound show in The Wizarding World of Harry Potter.

(2 Days) Getaway for Thrill-Seekers

Day 1: Universal Studios

Morning: Begin your adrenaline-fueled trip at Universal Studios Orlando, where adult tickets start at $115 and children's tickets start at $110. Rides like The Incredible Hulk Coaster and Hollywood Rip Ride Rockit will get your heart pounding.

Lunch: Recharge at Fast Food Boulevard in Springfield, where meals often cost $10 to $20 per person.

Afternoon: Immerse yourself in the world of cinematic magic with exciting attractions and entertaining entertainment.

Evening: Take in the bright ambiance of Universal CityWalk, which features a variety of dining, shopping, and entertainment options.

Day 2: Extravaganza at the Water Park

Morning: Cool down and have a good time in Volcano Bay, Universal's tropical water park, where admission costs around $80-85 per person. Relax on sandy beaches while riding the exhilarating water slides.

Lunch: Dine at Kohola Reef Restaurant & Social Club, where meals normally cost $10 to $20 per person.

Afternoon: Continue your water experiences to Volcano Bay, where you will find everything from peaceful winding rivers to exciting drop slides.

Evening: Relax at your hotel or explore Orlando's lively nightlife scene.

These sample itineraries provide an overview of the different experiences available in Orlando, ranging from charming theme parks to exhilarating water adventures. Feel free to customize them based on your choices and hobbies, ensuring that your Orlando holiday is personalized to your specific needs.

Theme Park Ticket Informations

Orlando is known as the ultimate theme park destination, with a dazzling selection of world-class attractions. Understanding the complexities of theme park ticket options and price is critical to making the most of your visit.

We provide thorough insights into ticketing, pricing structures, and value-added tips for a seamless theme park visit in this part.

Walt Disney World Resort

Walt Disney World Resort is made up of four separate theme parks: Magic Kingdom, Epcot, Disney's Hollywood Studios, and Disney's Animal Kingdom. Each park has its own distinct charm and attractions.

Tickets Types

Base Tickets: These provide entrance to a single park per day, with pricing varying depending on the day of your visit. Expect to pay between $109 to $159 for adults and $103 to $153 for children (ages 3 to 9).

Park Hopper Tickets: These tickets allow you to visit various parks on the same day. Adult prices range from $169 to $219, while children's prices range from $163 to $213.

Purchasing multi-day tickets frequently results in significant savings. A 4-day base ticket, for example, may cost roughly $89 per day for adults and $83 per day for children.

Pro Hints

- To ensure the greatest prices and availability, purchase your tickets well in advance, especially during peak holiday seasons.

- Package Deals: For potential cost savings, look at vacation packages that combine hotel accommodations, dining plans, and tickets.

Annual Passes: Frequent visitors may want to consider purchasing annual passes, which provide unrestricted park entrance as well as advantages such as eating and merchandise discounts.

Universal Orlando Resort

Universal Orlando Resort consists of Universal Studios Florida, Islands of Adventure, and Volcano Bay water park, each of which offers a variety of exhilarating activities.

Tickets Types

Base Tickets: A single-park ticket costs $115 for adults and $110 for children (ages 3-9). Ticket costs, like those at Disney, vary based on the day.

Park-to-Park Tickets: You can use these tickets to visit both Universal Studios Florida and Islands of Adventure on the same day. Adult prices range from $170 to $220, while children's prices range from $165 to $215.

Multi-Day Tickets: Universal sells multi-day tickets, with the cost per day decreasing as the number of days increases. A three-day park-to-park ticket might cost roughly $130 for adults and $125 for children.

Pro Hints

- Consider getting a Universal Express pass to skip typical lineups at some attractions, saving you significant time.

- Staying at a Universal Orlando Resort hotel allows you early park admission, giving you special access to select attractions.

- Keep an eye out for special events, such as Halloween Horror Nights, which may demand separate entry but provide unique experiences.

LEGOLAND Florida and SeaWorld Orlando

SeaWorld Orlando and LEGOLAND Florida, while not as large as Disney or Universal, provide wonderful experiences for families and guests of all ages.

Single-day tickets to SeaWorld Orlando start around $79.99 for adults and $74.99 for youngsters (ages 3-9). Check for seasonal promos and multi-park ticket discounts.

Tickets to LEGOLAND Florida start at $79.99 for adults and $74.99 for youngsters (ages 3-12).

Multi-day passes and combo tickets with LEGOLAND Water Park are frequently discounted.

- Before purchasing tickets, check the official websites of these parks for the most up-to-date prices, promotions, and any additional experiences or upgrades available.

In the competitive theme park landscape of Orlando, smart preparation and comprehension of your ticket options can make your visit not only memorable but also cost-effective.

Whether you are a Disney fan, a Universal fan, or looking for aquatic adventures, these tips will surely help you plan the best Orlando vacation possible yet.

Festivals and Annual Events

Orlando is a city that never stops celebrating, and it organizes a colorful assortment of annual events and festivals that cater to a wide range of interests throughout the year.

These events not only allow tourists to immerse themselves in the rich culture of the city, but they also provide unique and memorable experiences. Here's a detailed look at some of Orlando's most important annual events and festivals:

International Flower & Garden Festival at World's Epcot. (Spring)

Typically held between early March and late June.

Epcot's International Flower & Garden Festival transforms the park into a botanical wonderland as spring blooms. Stroll through finely maintained gardens filled with vivid flowers and topiaries of popular Disney characters.

Foodies will love the outdoor kitchens, which provide excellent seasonal cuisine and cool beverages. In addition, the American Gardens Theatre hosts live concerts by well-known musicians.

Admission: Epcot requires an admission ticket, and event-related activities are included with your park ticket.

Universal Orlando Resort's Halloween Horror Nights (Fall)

Typically, it runs on select nights between mid-September through October.

Halloween Horror Nights at Universal Orlando Resort is a must-see for those looking for spine-chilling thrills and shivers.

With lavishly decorated haunted houses, powerful fear zones, and pulse-pounding live entertainment, this event brings your worst nightmares to life.

Prepare to meet renowned horror movie characters and witness the pinnacle of haunted house architecture.

Entrance: Separate entrance is necessary, and tickets frequently sell out quickly, so it is best to get them ahead of time.

Mickey's Not-So-Scary Halloween Party at Magic Kingdom(Autumn)

Typically held on select nights between August and October.

Mickey's Not-So-Scary Halloween Party, ideal for families, promises a spooktacular evening of events at the historic Magic Kingdom park.

Adults and children alike can dress up in their favorite costumes and trick-or-treat throughout the park, collecting sweets and treats. This is a wonderful Halloween event with special parades, stage acts, and character meet-and-greets.

Admission: This is a separately ticketed event that must be paid in advance.

Fall Epcot International Food & Wine Festival at Walt Disney World

Typically, it occurs from late August until November.

During Epcot's International Food & Wine Festival, food aficionados and culinary enthusiasts revel. At the Global Marketplaces located around the park, you may sample delectable dishes and beverages from around the world.

Cooking demos by renowned chefs, wine and craft beer pairings, and live music performances are all available. This festival is a gourmet adventure unlike any other.

Tickets and Admission: Admission to Epcot is necessary, and also food and beverage sampling may incur additional fees.

Orlando Pride Festival At Downtown Orlando. (October)

Orlando Pride celebrations usually take place in early October.
Orlando Pride is a vibrant and welcoming celebration of the LGBTQ+ community. The Pride parade, which winds through downtown Orlando and features colourful floats, marching bands, and a varied assortment of participants, is the centerpiece.

The celebrations continue with a vibrant street festival including food, music, and a friendly spirit of acceptance and diversity.

Admission: While most events are free, certain activities and items may be charged.

International Film Festival of Orlando (November)

It usually lasts a few days in mid to late November at Various theaters and venues in and around Orlando.

The Orlando International Film Festival is a great place for film fans to pursue their love. This yearly event features independent and foreign films, giving budding filmmakers a platform and a varied spectrum of cinematic experiences.

Attend movies, participate in director conversations, so you can better understand and appreciate the art of storytelling through film.

Admission: Ticket costs vary based on the movies and events you attend.

Universal Orlando Resort's Mardi Gras (Spring)

Traditionally observed from February to early April.

With its Mardi Gras celebration, Universal Orlando Resort brings the essence of New Orleans to Florida. Enjoy a spectacular procession with intricately designed floats, enthusiastic performers, and bright costumes.

As you immerse yourself in the colorful ambiance of Mardi Gras, savor the Cajun cuisine, dance to live music, and catch some beads.

Tickets and Admission: admittance to Universal Studios Florida is necessary, and admittance to the Mardi Gras event is included with your park admission.

These annual events and festivals in Orlando would bring excitement and cultural diversity to your visit. When organizing your vacation, make sure to check the particular dates for each event, as they can vary somewhat from year to year.

Orlando has something for everyone, whether you are a foodie, a film enthusiast, or a fan of spectacular Halloween scares.

Printed in Great Britain
by Amazon

30869015R00094